THE FASHION LOVER'S GUIDE TO
MILAN

Dedication

To my mother, who loved the clothes and the cappuccinos,
and would have loved this book.

THE FASHION LOVER'S GUIDE TO
MILAN

RACHAEL MARTIN

WHITE OWL
AN IMPRINT OF PEN & SWORD BOOKS LTD.
YORKSHIRE - PHILADELPHIA

First published in Great Britain in 2021 by
PEN & SWORD WHITE OWL
An imprint of
Pen & Sword Books Ltd
Yorkshire - Philadelphia

ISBN 9781526733733

Printed and bound in India by Replika Press Pvt. Ltd.
Design: Paul Wilkinson.

Pen & Sword Books Limited incorporates the
imprints of Atlas, Archaeology, Aviation, Discovery,
Family History, Fiction, History, Maritime, Military,
Military Classics, Politics, Select, Transport,
True Crime, Air World, Frontline Publishing, Leo
Cooper, Remember When, Seaforth Publishing,
The Praetorian Press, Wharncliffe Local History,
Wharncliffe Transport, Wharncliffe True Crime and
White Owl.

For a complete list of Pen & Sword titles please
contact
PEN & SWORD BOOKS LIMITED
47 Church Street, Barnsley, South Yorkshire, S70 2AS,
United Kingdom
E-mail: enquiries@pen-and-sword.co.uk
Website: www.pen-and-sword.co.uk

Or
PEN AND SWORD BOOKS
1950 Lawrence Rd, Havertown, PA 19083, USA
E-mail: Uspen-and-sword@casematepublishers.com
Website: www.penandswordbooks.com

CONTENTS

FOREWORD

I FIRST CAME TO MILAN after I arrived in Italy at the end of the 1990s, with the soundtrack to the Merchant Ivory production of *A Room with View* still playing in my head and visions of that oh-so-seductive dolce vita. I spent my time getting on and off trains, eating pasta and pizza in every form I could find, and spending all my English language teacher's wages on clothes. I remember buying a pair of cream D&G jeans that first hot summer, and if you've ever been in Milan in summer, you'll understand how hot it can get. Not that I cared. I was in the city of the beautiful people buying a pair of cream D&G jeans, and I loved it all. I sat in cafés, cultivating a life-long appreciation of cappuccino and brioche. I studied the Italian girls and wondered how they managed to look just how they did. There was this Italian way of life that I could see playing out in front of my eyes, and I wanted a part of it. In the meantime, I was learning Italian. I was learning that language was a passport to culture, and that the only way I could really ever understand a culture was through its language.

Writing *A Fashion Lover's Guide to Milan* gave me the opportunity to write not only about the fashion, but also about a city through the lens of its fashion, a city I'd grown to love. Milan is one of the world's four fashion capitals. It's the Italian city that sent Italian fashion onto an international stage during the 1970s and 1980s. Just as Milan made Italian fashion so famous and desirable, fashion has helped to make Milan the city we see today. If I were to do this story any justice, I would have to include the bigger picture, to place fashion firmly within the city itself, and touch upon how Milan as a fashion city was created. If Milan is one of the world's fashion capitals today, it is because of all that went before. I also wanted to fill the guide with some of the places and people that have inhabited, and still do inhabit this world, and tell some of their stories, however briefly. These are

the stories that fascinated me, and continue to fascinate me. There are many Milanese fashion figures that are internationally famous, and then there are others, whose stories are not always so well known, and often women. They may be women you haven't heard of, or only heard of vaguely, but they are women whose stories equally deserve to be told.

By no means is this meant to be a fully comprehensive guide, but rather snapshots of a unique and fascinating world. You'll find different aspects of this world. Milan is a city of luxury fashion houses, but it's also home to much more, so alongside the designer names you'll find family-owned- businesses spanning several generations and creating artisan products such as jewellery, leather goods and accessories. There are the vintage fashion boutiques that provide inspiration for some of the world's top fashion designers, fashion students and fashion lovers alike. There are vintage markets, neighbourhood markets,

Adobe Stock

artisans producing homewares, and I've also included a few recommendations for children's clothing.

I've split the guide geographically, so each chapter focuses on a particular neighbourhood. Milan is a city of neighbourhoods each with its own distinct character. You'll also find recommendations for places of cultural interest, and for food. We're in Italy. Italy always involves recommendations for food. Besides, when you've been shopping all morning and you're tired and need a break, you need to know of a certain place that someone knows. Some of these places are high-end, while others are not. There is always a case for both.

If this is your first visit, start in the 'quadrilatero d'oro' or Golden Quad, Milan's luxury fashion district. Then make your way towards Brera with its boutiques and galleries, move towards the centre with its focal point of Piazza Duomo where the city's cathedral is, and take in some culture before heading for the boutiques and design places of Sant'Ambrogio and Corso Magenta. After that, the choice is yours. There's shopping beneath the skyscrapers of CityLife, along Corso Garibaldi, in Porta Nuova and up in Isola where the creatives live side by side with the locals. The canal area down around Porta Genova and Porta Ticinese offers a more alternative scene with vintage shops between the numerous bars and restaurants. Zona Tortona is the city's design district and home to the Armani/Silos, whose permanent exhibition is a fashion lover's dream, while Lambrate offers that neighbourhood vibe where Lambretta scooters were once made. In Milanese dialect they say 'Milan l'è un gran Milan' – literally, 'Milan is a great Milan' – and they are not wrong.

Give Milan your time, in spite of the fact that you might feel that time is what everyone else is lacking. That's normal. Milan is famous for its hard work ethic; it's how the Milanese get things done. Just look at the city's Duomo as an example. Go shopping. Visit the museums, sit in the cafés, walk along the streets of the different neighbourhoods. Go for an aperitivo. Listen to the sound of the language and absorb this city that has so much to share. Stay here for a while and you'll realise that Milan isn't just about the fashion or the design. It's about the whole Milanese experience.

If you're here for a long weekend, you won't see all of Milan by any means, but I hope you feel you can pick and choose and that you quickly wander off the more trodden tourist routes and explore some of the places mentioned in the book. Besides, you could always come back – and if you've never visited Milan when it's all dressed for Christmas, I strongly suggest you do.

One last thing: don't forget your sunglasses. Who cares if it's cloudy, this is Milan.

Acknowledgements

HEARTFELT THANKS TO everyone at the various fashion houses, museums, shops and other places included in the book who offered assistance and gave permission for photographs. To Janet Brookes, Karyn Burnham, Ester de Giuli, Antonella Meregalli, Alice Wright and Jonathan Wright.

Thank you also to Stefano, the other part of the reason I stayed, for taking his share, keeping us all fed and for making trays of fresh pasta when I needed it most.

MILAN, CITY OF FASHION

MILAN IS HOME to some of the world's most important fashion houses and hosts the Milan fashion weeks. As fashion capitals go, it's one of the big four, along with Paris, London and New York. It's the Italian city that sent Italian ready-to-wear out into the world in the latter quarter of the twentieth century. This is the fashion story that made Milan the fashion capital it is today. People such as Gianni Versace and his sister Donatella, Giorgio Armani, Gianfranco Ferré, Rosita and Ottavio Missoni, Valentino, Krizia, Walter Albini, Romeo

Gigli, Franco Moschino, Miuccia Prada, Domenico Dolce and Stefano Gabbana, Roberto Cavalli, and Tom Ford for Gucci all took part. Some, such as Giorgio Armani, Miuccia Prada, Domenico Dolce, Stefano Gabbana and Roberto Cavalli, are still living and working in Milan today. Fashion in Milan is everywhere. The city's luxury fashion district, known as the Golden Quad, has one of the highest concentrations of luxury boutiques in the world, and the fashion world's presence is seen throughout the city in cafés, restaurants, hotels and exhibition spaces.

It's a city with a fashion history that is fascinating. Its stories include that of Luisa Casati, who left Milan for Venice to live in the Palazzo Venier dei Leoni that then became home to the Peggy Guggenheim collection. There's Rosa Genoni, activist, proto-feminist, and one of the first advocates of Italian fashion in the early part of the twentieth century. Sisters Franca and Carla Sozzani each broke new ground in their own fields, and both encouraged innovation and young talents. Franca was *Vogue Italia* editor from 1988 until her death in 2016, and a style icon in her own right. She took the magazine away from the traditional fashion magazine with ground-breaking journalism and photography, while Carla, also a fashion editor and journalist, gave Milan its first concept store, the world-famous 10 Corso Como. There's the Curiel family,

four generations of women who have dressed so many ladies at the opening night of La Scala opera house. Germana Marucelli, another Milanese couturier, was originally from Settignano in Tuscany, and went to Milan in 1938[1] where she opened her atelier in Via Borgospesso, thanks to the generosity of loyal customer Flora d'Elys.[2] She became the post-war couturier that opened her Milanese home every Thursday to artists and writers such as Gio Ponti, although Milan has always fused fashion with culture and the arts. Anna Piaggi, muse of Karl Lagerfeld, milliner Stephen Jones and others, was the fashion journalist and visionary who made vintage a thing before anyone else was even looking at it. Fashion journalist Maria Pezzi recorded some of fashion history's greatest moments as she lived them.

The city's love of beautiful things dates back to the Renaissance, when clothing was a symbol of wealth and power, and good taste was beginning to be considered a quality. Milan was one of the main cities of the Renaissance. It flourished and became more powerful under the Visconti and Sforza dynasties, and just like in Florence and Mantua, this brought an emphasis on investment in the arts. Milan has a beauty that is not always immediately apparent. It doesn't shout its beauty; it's not showy or brashy. Rather, it's understated, and it's this understated quality that characterises Milanese

Rachael Martin

NOT JUST A FASHION CAPITAL...

Milan is also the Italian capital of design, and a city of contemporary arts, opera, business, publishing and more. Its history dates back to Roman times via French, Spanish and Austrian rule, and the Visconti and Sforza dynasties of the Renaissance. It's the city of St Ambrose or Sant'Ambrogio, Milan's patron saint and fourth-centruy Bishop of Milan, of Leonardo da Vinci's *The Last Supper* and Michelangelo's *RondanIni*

style and is visible in the city's various homes of illustrious Milanese figures throughout history and in the dress and homes of the Milanese today.

Naturally, the opportunities for serious shopping are everywhere. Whether you're into the iconic designer labels of Milan's luxury fashion district, the Golden Quad, prefer to explore the boutiques of Brera, concept stores such as 10 Corso Como, places with more of a street feel such as Porta Genova, or fancy investing in a bit of vintage couture, Milan has something for every taste. You only have to walk along Milan's streets to understand that fashion, and the concept of beauty, is something that is taken very seriously here. Beauty is all around you, in the boutiques, cafés, the elegant palazzos, the city's museums, and the way its people dress. In Milan it's a way of life, and it's that which makes the city so special and unique.

MILAN HAS A beauty that's all its own. It's courtyards glimpsed through gates as you're walking through the Sant'Ambrogio area or along Corso Venezia, or in other places around the historic centre. It's the sunset over the Navigilo Grande, the orange Carrelli tram making its way along Corso Magenta, the post-industrial buildings up in Lambrate and the view of the city from the Fondazione Prada's white concrete tower. Milan is a city that values its past while embracing its future, and the mix of styles of architecture that you see adds to its beauty and its appeal. You only have to look at the Piazza del Duomo. Where else can you see an Italian square that blends such different architectural periods to such stunning effect?

Pietà, and of the Fondazione Prada, the Armani/Silos and the Pirelli Hangar Bicocca. Urban regeneration during recent years in the Porta Nuova area has transformed its skyline with skyscrapers that now stand against the view of the Alps on a clear day. The CityLife district with its shopping centre has injected new life into the Milano Fiera area, and boasts towers by Zaha Hadid, Daniel Libeskind and Arata Isozaki, while its arts scene includes world-class venues such as the Fondazione Prada and the Pirelli HangarBicocca. Expo 2015 saw the theme of 'Feeding the Planet, Energy for Life,' appropriate in a city with such an exciting dining scene. It created new interest and a boom in tourism, and in 2019 the Global Destination Cities Index listed Milan as the sixteenth most visited city in the world – and the only Italian city listed in the top twenty.

MILAN FASHION WEEK

Milan Fashion Week takes its place among the big four: New York, London, Milan and Paris, which happen in that order. Legendary Fashion Week stories tell of a whole city brimming and buzzing with designers, models, journalists, photographers and buyers, along with the often famous clientele and those all-important fashion editors. Stories of tensions abound with clothes being changed right at the last minute. The shows are organised by the Camera Nazionale della Moda Italiana (National Chamber of Italian Fashion), which has been promoting Italian fashion since 1958. Creative directors put their creations on the catwalks and on digital platforms, while the Fashion Hub Market showcases twelve emerging designers. Note that hotels fill up quickly and prices do go up, so it's advisable to book early.

If you're not one of the lucky few to manage to get an invite to the shows, events and parties with famous guests and all the best DJs – and let's face it, the majority of us aren't – you can still enjoy Fashion Week nevertheless. Look for outside shows in historic places such as Piazza del Duomo and the grounds of the Sforza Castle. Vogue for Milano, previously known as Vogue Fashion's Night Out, is the event that takes place every September in conjunction with the Comune di Milano and gives the general public the opportunity to participate. It's a celebration of fashion within a city and a consolidation of that city's relationship with fashion, so head out and soak up that fashion atmosphere. Shops in the centre are open till late and there are events and shopping experiences within the Golden Quad, including initiatives that aim to give something back to young people through education and other projects. There are also art and photography exhibitions, and music, in particular live concerts in Piazza del Duomo. For information, check Vogue Italia for a list of events. (**www.vogue.it**) The September Fashion Week also hosts the Fashion Film Festival showing short films by emerging directors, all linked by theme.

Fashion Week Dates

Womenswear – February for fall/winter collections and September for spring/summer

Menswear – January for fall/winter collections and June for spring/summer

For further information, see
www.cameramoda.it

THE HISTORY OF THE ITALIAN FASHION SHOWS

Right up until the Second World War, Paris dominated the fashion scene. Roman-born Elsa Schiaparelli was guiding fashion during the 1930s alongside Chanel,[3] but she was living and working in Paris and her couture was made in France. Paris enabled Schiaparelli to gain the recognition that wouldn't have been possible in other countries, including Italy.[4] The Italians were known for accessories, mainly Salvatore Ferragamo shoes. Even when the years of fascism brought economic isolation, Italian couturiers still looked to the French for their inspiration.[5] When war broke out and it became impossible to import French designs, Italy was forced to look to itself, and after the war for ways to rebuild its economy. It was this that led to the beginnings of fashion that could be called Italian.[6]

This is when an astute Florentine aristocrat and businessman named Giovanni Battista Giorgini stepped in. Giorgini had already been exporting artisan homeware to the various buyers within the American department stores, and after the war he decided to do the same thing with fashion. On 12 February 1951 he held the first Italian fashion show at his Florentine home, Villa Torrigiani, to promote Italian fashion to an international market. Of course fashion shows were nothing new, but this was staged with the specific marketing purpose of presenting Italian fashion to foreign buyers.[7] The nine Alta Moda couturiers included Simonetta Visconti, the Fontana Sisters, Germana Marucelli and Veneziani.[8] Giorgini also presented four boutique designers that included Emilio Pucci.[9] Boutique wear was a more relaxed way of dressing that appealed to an American market and a post-war culture. It was new, it was fresh, it was a thoroughly modern concept of fashion, and it was something that Paris wasn't doing. In addition, it cost half the price of French fashion.[10] The fashion show was a success and attracted attention from international press.[11]

The Italian High Fashion shows had begun, and the year after, in July 1952, Giorgini held a show at the Sala Bianca in Palazzo Pitti, home to the Uffizi Galleries and a highly prestigious venue in Florence. The setting was in one of the rooms where parties were held in one of Florence's most beautiful palazzos, with the Boboli Gardens behind, and was perfect for the Alta Moda and boutique creations on display. Yet Florence still didn't become a focal point for fashion in the way Milan would later. The Roman couture houses asked for, and got, their own programme of fashion shows.[12] Fashion in Italy was still spread across several cities, including Milan, Venice and Turin, and not yet gathered in one fashion capital.

In 1958 the 'Camera Sindicale della Moda Italiana' was set up in Rome for the promotion and development of fashion, which then became the 'Camera Nazionale della Moda Italiana', or National Chamber of Italian Fashion. The same year saw the first Milan fashion show in Via Gattamelata.

In 1978 Beppe Modenese organized Modit, a trade fair of ready-to-wear factory-made designer clothing, with designers such as Walter Albini, Laura, Biagiotti and Ken Scott. Others including Versace and Ferré joined, and the shows became known as Centro Sfilate, literally, centre for the fashion shows.[13] This would then become Milano Collezioni. According to fashion journalist Maria Pezzi, Florence had opened the door with Pucci, knitwear and boutique fashion, and Milan pushed it wide open.[14]

Shows take place each day during the week, in various venues and on digital platforms. Some fashion houses have their own private theatres, while others rent various locations around the city. Milan isn't the only Italian city that has its fashion shows, although obviously only Milan takes its place amid the four fashion capitals. Rome's Altaroma is an important platform for emerging designers. Pitti Immagine in Florence started as Pitti Uomo and now encompasses various collections including childrenswear and knitting yarn collections, while Venice's Fashion Week places the emphasis on slow fashion and gives priority to the sartorial and ethical.

MUSEUMS

Milan is also about the arts and is home to many important museums as diverse as the Pinacoteca di Brera, Fondazione Prada and the Armani/ Silos. Fashion houses give back to the city through arts projects and world-class venues and exhibitions. For example, the Nicola Trussardi Foundation, chaired by Beatrice Trussardi, promotes contemporary art and culture by way of exhibitions and installations throughout Milan. Design Week 2019 saw their huge installation, 'A Friend', by Ghanaian artist Ibrahim Mahama, which covered the Porta Venezia Neoclassical tollgates with themes of diversity and integration. Milan's Salone Internazionale del Mobile, the city's furniture fair, takes place during Design Week and fuses design with the worlds of fashion, art and food. Watch out for spectacular installations in boutiques and fashion houses all over the city, and in its museums and art galleries. The city also hosts the yearly Photo Vogue Festival in November, which includes fashion photography. See Vogue Italia **www.vogue.it** for details.

Armani/Silos *(see page 173)*
With around 600 works, four floors, a digital archive plus temporary design and photography exhibitions, it really is as beautiful as you would expect.

Fondazione Prada

Visit the Fondazione Prada to see how the world of fashion has contributed to the world of the arts in one of Milan's most prestigious contemporary art spaces. Fondazione Prada is a cultural institution that was established in Milan by Miuccia Prada and Patrizio Bertelli in 1993. The project of the permanent venue by architect Rem Koolhaas opened in 2015 and is located in what was once an early twentieth-century distillery in an industrial area of Milan. It combines existing buildings with three new structures: Podium, Cinema and Torre. There's the Haunted House covered in gold leaf, while the Torre is the 60-metre-high white concrete tower that houses the Atlas project, which arose from a dialogue between Miuccia Prada and Germano Celant and contains works from the Prada collection such as Carsten Höller's *Mushrooms* and Jeff Koons's *Tulips*. On the sixth floor, you'll find the Torre Restaurant that combines art and design furniture, and offers an Italian menu that draws on regional influences. The foundation hosts both permanent and temporary art exhibitions along with performances, film screenings and other events. Also visit the deliciously retro 'Bar Luce', designed by Wes Anderson, which recreates a typical bar from mid-twentieth-century Milan, with pinball machines, jukebox and Formica tables. The roof is a mini recreation of that in the Galleria Vittorio Emanuele.

Fondazione Prada, Largo Isarco, 2, 02 5666 2611, Mon/Wed/Thurs 10 am – 7 pm, Fri/Sat/Sun 10 am – 9 pm; Bar Luce, Largo Isarco, 2, 02 5666 2611, Mon/Wed/Thurs 9 am – 8 pm, Fri/Sat/Sun 9 am – 9 pm. **www.fondazioneprada.org**

Fondazione Gianfranco Ferré

(see page 174)
Original concept sketches, clothing, jewellery and objects from the designer's life. You need to book in advance, but it's a fascinating place for fashion students and serious fashion lovers.

Fondazione Prada. Bas Princen, courtesy of Fondazione Prada

Palazzo Morando Costume Moda Immagine *(see page 40)*
Milan's museum of fashion and costume has a rotating permanent collection, and hosts temporary exhibitions.

Palazzo Reale *(see page 94)*
Past exhibitions have involved fashion and fashion photography. It's also a venue for the Photo Vogue Festival. Check what's on before you go.

Pirelli HangarBicocca
This contemporary art space is on the outskirts of Milan in the former industrial district of Bicocca in what was once a locomotive factory. Temporary exhibitions take place alongside the permanent exhibition of Anselm Kiefer's 'The Seven Heavenly Palaces 2004–2015', which was commissioned for its opening in 2004. The aim is to give art to the people, along with cultural events, talks, films and music. Admission is free.

Pirelli HangarBicocca, Via Chiese, 2, 02 6611 1573, Thurs–Sun 10 am – 10 pm.
www.pirellihangarbicocca.org

TRIENNALE MILANO

Triennale Milano opened as a Triennal International exhibition about design and decorative arts in 1933 in Milan's Palazzo dell'Arte, and was built by the architect Giovanni Muzio. It is an international institution that brings together all forms of contemporary culture: design, fashion, architecture, urban planning, the visual arts, new media, photography, performance, theatre, dance, and music. It's a place where art and design, creativity and technology, tradition and innovation all interact. It also organizes the Triennale di Milano International Exhibition, one of the most important design and architecture events, which was revived in 2016 after a twenty-year hiatus.

Design Week 2019 saw the inauguration of a new permanent ground-floor exhibition, the Museum of Italian Design. The iconic pieces on show are drawn from the museum's 1,600-piece design collection and cover the history of design from just after the Second World War to 1981. This is 'episode one', the golden years of design, as president of the museum and architect Stefano Boeri explained when it opened, the first part of a larger project that will give Milan a museum dedicated solely to Italian design. Check what's on before you go.

Triennale di Milano, Viale Emilio Alemagna, 6, 02 724341, Tues–Sun 10.30 am – 8.30 pm. **www. triennale.org**

Finally, don't forget the Valentino Garavini 3D virtual museum. **www. valentinogaravanimuseum.com**

ALSO VISIT...
Ago, Filo e Nodo
Ago, Filo e Nodo (Needle, Thread and Knot) is the sculpture in two parts

Beatrice d'Este's slipper: female shoe in decorated leather found inside the Castle of Vigevano, end of 15th century.
MIC Museo Internazionale della Calzatura "P.Bertolini" - Vigevano

created by Claes Oldenburg and Coosje van Bruggen. It's a tribute to Milan's fashion industry and can be seen outside Cadorna station in Piazzale Cadorna.

OUT OF TOWN

Museo Internazionale della Calzatura Pietro Bertolini, Vigevano

This international shoe museum is a mere half an hour's train ride away in the pretty provincial town of Vigevano. When Christian Dior presented his New Look in 1947, it was revolutionary and became emblematic of a new Europe after the austerity of war and the utilitarian clothing associated with it. Scarcity of material gave way to cinched waists that announced the fullest of skirts. A New Look needed a new shoe and preferably a high heel, yet wooden heels tended to break. In January 1953 several local businesses each presented their shoes at the town's international shoe fair. The shoes had stiletto heels, made out of both wood and aluminium and with a 6–7cm heel. The New Look now had its new shoe, and Vigevano

became the world shoe capital. Manolo Blahnik shoes are also produced here in the town, shoes that have become fashion icons and which for some of us will be forever connected with Carrie Bradshaw and *Sex and the City*.

The museum arose from the personal

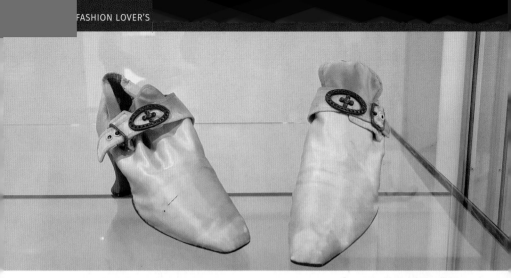

Poiret "Richelieu" slipper with strap and buckle and central oval decoration. Spool heel in red satin. Leather sole. Material: ivory satin. Origin: France 1905.
MIC Museo Internazionale della Calzatura "P.Bertolini" - Vigevano

collection of Pietro Bertolini, who began collecting shoes and relevant items and documents back in the 1930s, and the resulting collection reads like a history of the shoe. Visit the 'Stanza della Duchessa' (the Room of the Duchess), the duchess being Beatrice D'Este, who married Ludovico Sforza when she was only 15 years old. Beatrice was a Renaissance fashion icon, famous throughout the European courts for her style, and the museum's most precious piece is a pair of shoes worn by her during her time at the Sforza Castle in Milan at the end of the fifteenth century. Ladies' shoes during the Renaissance were really slippers, made from fine leather, silk or velvet, and this example is all the more precious because of its rarity. The museum itself is housed in another castle where Beatrice spent time, the Castello Sforzesco in Vigevano.

Futurist sandal: two-coloured strap sandal, coloured wooden spools. Anonymous, donation from Bertolini. Materials: leather, blue and yellow wood, c. 1940, inspired by the artistic current of Futurism.

In fact, the Loggia delle Dame, or Ladies' Loggia, was built for Beatrice.

The museum has examples of shoes from the eighteenth and nineteenth centuries that include 1920s models by French fashion designer Paul Poiret who was a favourite designer of Luisa Casati. (He made her famous 'fountain dress'.) There are shoes from the years of fascism when materials were scarce and shoe designers were forced to be inventive – think Salvatore Ferragamo and his cork wedges – as well as shoes from right through the second half of the twentieth century. Other shoes include those made for celebrities such as Marilyn Monroe, sports shoes from the 1920s - 1950s, and shoes made by leading designers such as Christian Lacroix, Christian Louboutin and Manolo Blahnik.

Museo Internazionale della Calzatura Pietro Bertolini, Castello Sforzesco, Vigevano, 0381 693952, Tues–Fri 2 – 5.30 pm, Sat–Sun 10 am – 6 pm. **www.museocalzaturavigevano.it**

Museo della Seta, Como

Milan is also near Lake Como, giving you the opportunity to combine a visit to the city with a visit to the lake. Head to the town of Como, which is internationally famous for silk production, and about an hour away from Milan. It was Ludovico Sforza, Duke of Milan during the fifteenth century, who originally planted mulberry trees around Lake Como, from which silk worms fed. A visit to the silk museum here not only gives you the chance to explore all aspects of silk production but will also help you to appreciate the weight of local industry behind the fashion and the fact that this was all being made to the highest quality. It's the only museum in the world to show the production process from silk worm to finished

The city of Como at the south-western tip of Lake Como.

yarn. You'll also get to view some stunning examples of clothes.

Museo della Seta, Via Castelnuovo, 9, Como, 031 303 180, Tues – Sat 10 am – 6 pm. **www.museosetacomo.com**

Parco Teresio Olivelli in Tremezzina (Como) is where Dolce & Gabbana held their Alta Moda show in July 2018. The event was an exotic and bohemian interpretation of Alessandro Manzoni's 1827 novel *The Betrothed*, complete with costumed 'Alessandro Manzoni' signing copies of his classic book that helped to form the foundation for modern Italian culture.

Parco Teresio Olivelli, Via Statale 47, Tremezzo

Also go to Lopez vintage before you go home. It's a treasure trove of vintage clothing and accessories with an impressive archive from past centuries.

Lopez Vintage, Via Vitani, 26, Como, 031 242043, Tues - Sat 10 am - 7 pm

VINTAGE FASHION

Milan's vintage scene encompasses all the biggest names in Italian and international fashion, and recent years have seen a significant increase in terms of sales, the number of vintage shops and the various markets around the city. You might come across Italian fashion names such as Germana Marucelli or Curiel, who dressed so many ladies attending the opening nights at La Scala opera house. There are the three Fontana Sisters, brought up in the family tailoring shop who left their small town near Parma and went to Rome where they dressed Italian princesses and American film stars. There's Maria Antonelli, whose designs foresaw the minimalism of the 1960s, Jole Veneziani who played a major role in the rise of Made in Italy, tailor to the stars Emilio Schuberth, and Florentine aristocrat Emilio Pucci, the prince of prints. Alberto Fabiani was born into a family of couturiers and married another couturier, Simonetta, who came from a family of Sicilian aristocrats. Biki dressed Maria Callas and turned her into a diva. Irene Galitzine, from Georgia and the daughter of a prince, fled during the 1917 October Revolution and went to Italy. She became known for what Diana Vreeland called her 'palazzo pyjamas', while Walter Albini was a key figure in the rise of luxury prêt-à-porter. Italian fashion history is an impressive force. Designers, fashion stylists, fashion photographers and fashion students – you'll find them all hanging out in Milan's vintage shops, looking for inspiration or researching a particular look or technique.

Whether you're looking for a 1970s dress for that summer event or Christmas party, a vintage handbag, or have a thing about vintage jewellery, start looking and don't just limit yourself to names you've heard of. There were a lot of Italian dressmakers during the middle of the last century who were making beautiful tailor-made garments with high quality fabrics. Names to look out for with regards to handbags include both Pirovano and Roberta di Camerino. Of course not all of us can stretch to vintage couture, but there's also a good selection of shops that sell more recent pieces at more affordable prices, including second-hand clothing.

Vintage-inspired: La Double J

For a colourful retro style, check out La Double J, which you can find online at **www.ladoublej.com**. La Double J is the label founded by J.J. Martin in 2015. California-born, Martin has lived in Milan for nearly twenty years. She started with dresses, added homeware, childrenswear, and in 2019 launched her 'Goddess Collection', where the message is very much about female empowerment. Colour is key, and patterns are mainly sourced from vintage prints and wallpapers, and all is exclusively made in Italy.

THE FASHION LOVER'S LIST: VINTAGE FASHION

1. **20134 Lambrate.** A vintage treasure trove below the barber's shop sign in Lambrate (See page 181)

2. **Ambroeus.** Quality second-hand and vintage clothing in the heart of the Isola neighbourhood (See page 147)

3. **Cavalli e Nastri.** With one shop in Brera, and two in the Porta Ticinese area, they have a wide selection of vintage clothing and accessories (See page 78)

4. **Lipstick Vintage.** Clothing and accessories from the whole of the twentieth century, alongside eighteenth- and nineteenth-century displays (See page 137)

5. **Madame Pauline.** Clothes, jewellery, hats, stoles and other accessories from the early twentieth century onwards (See page 81)

6. **Pourquoi Moi.** Scandinavian cottons alongside sartorial and designer pieces (See page 162)

7. **Vintage Delirium by Franco Jacassi.** Legendary vintage shop renowned for its huge selection of buttons, clothes, fabrics and embroidery (See page 83)

To book a private shopping appointment in the showroom at Piazza Arcole, 4, see the website. **www.ladoublej.com**

VINTAGE MARKETS AND EVENTS

Check the various websites and Facebook pages for dates of events. Some are in Italian, but dates are always clear nevertheless.

Chez Babette Garage Sale

Monthly garage sale at the Autofficina Ferrante Vito, a working garage up in Lambrate where private sellers offer a selection of clothing and accessories including vintage, second hand, artisan-made and sneakers.

Chez Babette Garage Sale, Autofficina Ferrante Vito, Via Wildt, 2. See their Facebook and Instagram pages @chezbabettegaragesale for dates.

East Market

The hugely popular East Market is inspired by East London markets, where private individuals and professionals sell all that is vintage including 1990s clothing, vinyl, sneakers and much more. The market is slightly out of the centre, so you'll need to hop on tram number 27 from the centre. Make more of a day of it and head for the food trucks for lunch, an aperitivo or dinner with a plastic-free policy. Entry is 3 euro, under 14s enter free. Also visit their shop in Porta Venezia.

East Market, via Mecenate, 88/A, **www.eastmarketmilano.com**

East Market. LUDIDAX

East Market Shop, Via Bernardino Ramazzini, 6, 02 36588037, Mon 2.30pm – 7.30pm, Tues-Sat 10.30 am – 7.30 pm, Fri-Sun 10.30 am – 8 pm

Frida Market

Frida Market takes place at Frida in the Isola district. Go for clothing, vintage fashion, artisan made products and vinyl.

Frida Market, Frida, Via Antonio Pollaiuolo, 3 (see page 146)

Mercatone dell'Antiquariato

Monthly antiques market that takes place along the Naviglio Grande with around 400 market stalls selling antiques, vintage clothing, mid-century furniture and more.

Mercatone dell'Antiquariato, Naviglio Grande (see page 168)

Next Vintage Castello di Belgioioso

Next Vintage is the twice-yearly event that takes place in April and October and sees Castello di Belgioioso brought to life with vintage clothing, accessories and remade furniture and design. It's south of Milan, just past Pavia on the way to Cremona. If you're a vintage-lover and just happen to be in Milan on the right weekend, it's definitely worth a visit.

Next Vintage, Castello di Belgioioso, **www.belgioioso.it/vintage**

Wunder Markt

Clothing, graphics, design, artisan products, food, workshops, kids' areas and more that takes place in various other locations.

See Facebook @wundermarkt for details.

MILAN, CITY OF FASHION: A HISTORICAL GUIDE

The 1950s and early 1960s

During the 1950s and the first years of the 1960s, clothing was a clear indicator of who you were.[15] High fashion was made by couturiers and dressmakers who produced sartorial fashion and sartorial boutique fashion. What distinguished the wardrobe of the Milanese signora were high quality fabrics and expert craftsmanship, and also the added accessories. It was this that defined the true signora, and it was this that the couturier Biki taught Maria Callas via the handwritten notes she would write for her to tell her exactly what to wear with what. Creating a diva involved creating a signora, and what marked out the signora was how she put together her dress with her accessories. Every signora had her favourite dressmaker, if not her preferred couturier. Milan's great couturiers included Biki, Germana Marucelli, Gigliola Curiel and Mila Schön. Their clientele was generally rooted within a world of fashion that included aristocrats, industrialists and politicians. It revolved around society events, of which the opening night at La Scala opera house was generally considered to be the most important. Milan has always loved its opera house, right from the days when it was first built towards the end of the eighteenth century by decree of Empress Maria Teresa of Austria.[16]

Italy's post-war austerity of the 1950s led to the boom years of the 1960s, which were particularly felt in Milan. There were Fiat cars, Lambretta scooters made in Milan's Lambrate district by Innocenti, Olivetti typewriters and domestic appliances. At the end of the 1960s, the new youth generation began to seek freedom from the old cultural norms represented by a traditionalist society. This new youth culture found itself a voice through music, art and fashion. Swinging London was making itself heard and seen with groups such as The Beatles and boutiques such as Biba and Mary Quant's Bazaar. Boutiques such as Gulp and Cose had opened on Via della Spiga, bringing all the latest English and French boutique fashion to Milan.[17] People flocked to a store named Fiorucci, which had opened in May 1967. Elio Fiorucci brought London fashion to a Milanese audience, making it more widely available.

1968

1968 brought social and political change on a global scale, with heavy losses of life during the Vietnam War, civil rights' protests, the assassination of Martin Luther King, the Prague Spring, and the Paris riots in May and occupation of the Sorbonne. In Italy, Milan was the city where 1968 was felt most, and protests took place against the old orders of tradition and authority. Prestigious schools such as Parini and Berchet were occupied as was the University of Milan, and the University of Milan's students' movement led by Mario Capanna is considered to have been the most powerful and influential of the students' movements. The Triennale Art and Design Museum was occupied by artists that included brothers Gio and Arnaldo Pomodoro, while Capanna and his students' movement blocked Via Solferino, home to the Italian newspaper *Corriere della Sera*. When, on 7 December, Capanna and the students' movement threw eggs at the evening gowns, furs and dinner jackets of the people attending the opening night of La Scala, the students weren't protesting against La Scala as such, but against what they considered the traditionalist and oppressive society of the politicians, Milanese bourgeoisie and wealthy industrialists that attended it. 'Sessantotto' as 1968 is always referred to in Italian, signalled the fight for social equality which also led to the birth of the feminist movements. The traditional female confines of marriage and home were viewed as bourgeois on an intellectual level, and perceived as stifling by many. As women fought for equal rights within the home, the right to leave the confines of the home, the right to divorce and to legally access abortion, they also sought freedom through their clothes. (Divorce became legal in 1970 and abortion in 1978.) Milan was undergoing significant changes and this provided fertile ground for changes within fashion.

1971 and Made in Italy

The main centre for these changes in fashion was Milan. The exhibition 'Italiana. L'Italia vista dalla moda 1971–2001', curated by Maria Luisa Frisa and Stefano Tonchi took place at Milan's Palazzo Reale in 2018, and dates the beginning of Italian luxury ready-to-wear as 1971. This was when Walter Albini's fashion show took place in April, in the midst of an unfolding cultural landscape that would bring yet more change and new ways of self-expression. Albini had been making prêt-à-porter fashion already at the end of the 1960s, inspired by the grand couturiers of the 1920s and 1930s. When he chose to present his first prêt-à-porter collection under his own name, it was significant that he didn't choose Florence but Milan.[18] Albini's show heralded a new era in fashion, and of self-expression through prêt-à-porter clothing for both men and women that was androgynous and reflected the spirit of the time and the request for equality. It broke away from the previous canons of style embodied by the world of haute couture. The term ready-to-wear may have been coined by the Americans, but the Italians used the French term, which they took from French couturier Yves Saint Laurent, who opened his prêt-à-porter boutique, Rive Gauche, in 1966. Albini also signified a further change. He is regarded by many as the first modern designer as his was the first show that focused on industrially produced designer clothes. The couturiers of the past would give way to the designers of the future, with Made in Italy luxury prêt-à-porter fashion, and Milan as the heartland of that fashion. Albini, Krizia and Missoni were all some of the first designers involved in such a change.[19]

The rise of Made in Italy

What was becoming clear was that fashion design and the industry could be one and the same, and industry played a role in producing prêt-à-porter and in encouraging new talent. Walter Albini worked with textiles company Etro. Gianni Versace arrived in Milan from Reggio Calabria in 1972 and in 1973 started designing for, among others, Byblos, one of the labels created by manufacturer Genny. Walter Albini, Gianni Versace and Romeo Gigli all designed for Callaghan. Giorgio Armani came to Milan from Piacenza in the mid 1960s, and initially worked as a window dresser at La Rinascente. In 1975 he formed his own company with Sergio Galeotti, and showed his first collection for men and women; in 1982 he would grace the cover of *Time* magazine with 'Giorgio's Gorgeous Style'. Versace followed in 1978 with his first women's collection. Krizia and Gianfranco Ferré were others who took centre stage. Something was

happening in Milan, and it was different to the Roman couture represented by couturiers such as Valentino: this was high quality prêt-à-porter fashion.

The textiles industry upon which it all depended stretched not only throughout the Milan area, but also across northern Italy, with woollens from Biella, silk from Como, knitwear from Treviso and buttons from Bergamo. This history of quality textiles ran alongside a tradition of tailoring and a strong work ethic in family-run businesses. Plus, Milan had an infrastructure unlike any other Italian city, as well as airports. It was the centre for publishing, advertising and the fashion press. *Grazia, Gioia, Annabella* and *Amica* magazines were based there. Condé Nast bought a magazine called *Novità* in 1962. It became *Vogue Italia* in 1966, while *L'Uomo Vogue*, originally an insert of *Vogue Italia* became an independent magazine from 1967. Fashion magazines were crucial because they were interpreting fashion and the designers in new ways that started to break with tradition. Milan had everything going for it, and would become one of the greatest fashion capitals in the world as 'Made in Italy' brands moved out of the 1970s and into the 1980s and onto an international stage. Giorgio Armani revolutionised the suit and gave a new generation of women a working wardrobe: shirt, jacket and a pair of trousers, and there you were, all ready for the office. On a cultural level, it was a symbol of androgyny and a reach for gender equality in the boardroom.

1990s
The 1990s brought a golden age in Italian fashion. The vision of Franca Sozzani, legendary *Vogue Italia* editor, pushed boundaries and fused fashion with provocative social themes. Sozzani believed that fashion came from a social, political and economic time, and as such reflected this in her work. It was the time of the supermodels, credited as the creation of Sozzani along with photographers such as Steven Meisel, Peter Lindbergh and Bruce Weber. In 1990 Tom Ford was appointed creative director of Gucci, one of a new generation of international creative directors. Ford seduced Generation X fashionistas, and gained a seal of approval from Madonna that made Gucci the label everyone wanted after she wore it to the MTV video music awards in 1995.[20] There was grunge and then there was Tom Ford glamour and sexual allure, and Gucci was a brand that was Italian and associated with quality. With Tom Ford, Gucci moved into fashion, just as Prada did under Miuccia Prada. Both were companies that previously made luxury accessories. Prada subverted Milanese good taste while still retaining its appeal to that same Milanese sense of style, Dolce & Gabbana expounded the 'Sicilian woman' look and explored Sicilian textile traditions, and Versace provided all-out sex appeal and glamour in exquisite

fabrics. Giorgio Armani took everything that encapsulated Milanese taste and made it the hallmark of Italian style.

Yet when you walk along the streets of Milan's Golden Quad, in spite of all the luxury and the glamour it represents, it still retains that sense of Milanese understated elegance. It might not seem that way on a busy Saturday afternoon with the tourists and those who have come in for the day. (The Milanese are generally off in ski resorts like Courmayeur, or in second homes along the Ligurian Riviera, depending on the season.) Yet try walking down one of the quieter streets on a cold December evening when the Christmas lights have been switched on. All is surprisingly quiet, yet you know that up in the palazzos private sales are taking place, and in another room someone is showing next season's collection. The only thing that's showy is in the shop windows, and maybe a few tourists laden down with shopping bags. The rest is typically Milanese.

Adobe Stock

Rosa Genoni (fourth from right) at the International Congress of Women at The Hague, 1915.
Public domain https://www.flickr.com/people/35128489@N07

ROSA GENONI

Rosa Genoni is remembered for her efforts and commitment within the world of fashion and activism. Born in Tirano in 1867, at the age of 10 she was sent to Milan as a 'piscinina', as girls who were apprentices to seamstresses were known in the industry at the time. While she was learning and later qualifying as a master seamstress, she learned French, which at the time was the international language of fashion;[21] and also became interested in politics. In 1984, she was sent to Paris as a delegate of the Italian Workers' Party and stayed there for a while to perfect her techniques. Genoni designed for the most prestigious Milanese fashion house of the time, H. Haardt e Fils, and became a designer in her own right. She taught dressmaking and the history of fashion for the Women's Professional School at the Humanitarian Society in Milan until 1933, when she left her teaching position because she refused to swear her loyalty to fascism. She was a socialist, pacifist, an advocate for women's working conditions and the protection of minors, a writer for the socialist paper *L'Avanti*, and represented Italy at the International Congress of Women at The Hague in 1915. Genoni is also known for her work at the San Vittore prison in Milan, where she set up a sewing workshop for the women.

At a time when Paris firmly held its position as the centre of the fashion world, Genoni believed in the potential of Italian fashion. Her famous dress designs include the works she presented at Milan Expo in 1906, inspired by Renaissance painters such as Pisanello and Botticelli and his *Primavera*, where she showed Italian fabrics and craftsmanship to the world. Her Tanagra dress, which she designed for the actress Lyda Borelli, made a powerful statement. Significantly, it was inspired by mortal women, not the goddesses shown in the Tangara figurines, and was draped and fluid in contrast with the corseted shapes of the time. She is considered a feminist before her time, because she saw that clothing didn't necessarily have to restrict a woman, but that it could be a way for her to express herself.[22]

1 The Golden Quad

2 Brera

3 Duomo

4 Sant'Ambrogio

5 Corso Magenta

6 CityLife Shopping District

7 Porta Venezia

8 Corso Buenos Aires

9 Porta Nuova (Piazza Gae Aulenti)

10 Corso Como

11 Corso Garibaldi

12 Isola

13 Via Paola Sarpi

14 Porta Genova

15 Porta Ticinese

16 Navigli

17 Zona Tortona

18 Lambrate – four metro stops east on the M2 (green line) from Centrale

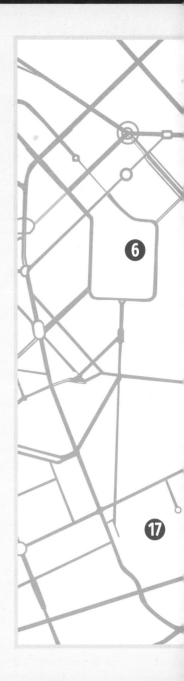

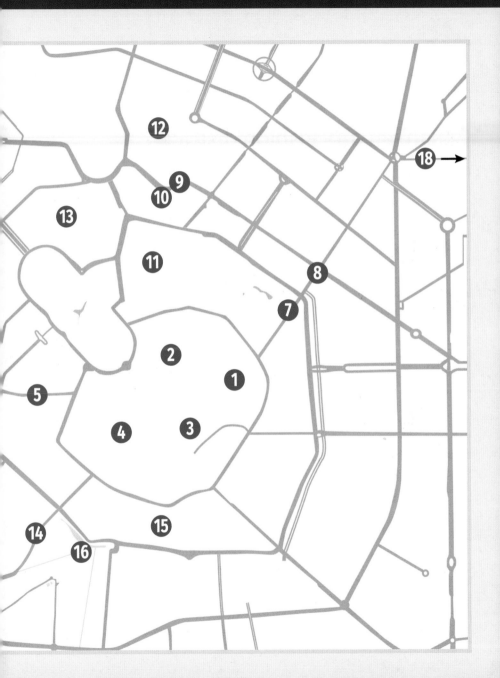

1

THE GOLDEN QUAD:
Milan's luxury fashion district

M1 San Babila/Palestro • M3 Montenapoleone

MILAN'S GOLDEN QUAD or Fashion Quad is the luxury fashion district that's a must-visit on any fashion lover's list. It's the shopping ground of the rich and often famous, including Hollywood celebrities, rock stars, European aristocrats, Middle Eastern royalty and more. It formed the backdrop for a golden age in Italian fashion with the rise of Italian ready-to-wear during the 1970s, leading to its heyday in the 1980s and 90s. This is where Giorgio Armani built his empire from Via Borgonuovo and where Gianni Versace welcomed stars from the world of film and music to Palazzo Versace in Via Gesù. It's your fashion dream, one of the highest concentrations of luxury boutique and flagship stores in the world, where you can literally walk out of one designer boutique into another right next door.

So why is it known as the Golden Quad? Firstly, because it contains so many luxury boutiques, and because it's literally a quadrangle marked out by the streets of Via Montenapoleone, Via Manzoni, Via della Spiga and Corso

Venezia. This quadrangle contains various streets within it, such as Via Sant'Andrea, Via Borgospesso, Via Sant Spirito, Via Gesù and Via Bagutta. The history of the area dates back to Roman times, when Milan was a city known as Mediolanum, and Massimiano chose to make it the capital of his empire and imperial residence. Via Manzoni follows the route of the old Roman road that led out to the Roman Porta Nuova at the crossroads where Via Borgnuovo and Via Montenapoleone meet, while Via Montenapoleone follows the course of what used to be the Roman walls.

QUADRILATERAL. 1 Balenciaga, 2 Dior, 3 Dolce & Gabbana, 4 Emilio Pucci, 5 Gucci, 6 Prada, 7 Roberto Cavalli, 8 Salvatore Ferragamo, 9 Valentino, 10 Versace, 11 Curiel, 12 Gio Moretti, 13 Pretty Ballerinas, 14 Giorgio Armani, 15 Banner, 16 Bottega Veneta, 17 Giambattista Valli, 18 Missoni, 19 Miu Miu, 20 Moschino, 21 Brioni, 22 Babba Napoli, 23 Doucal's, 24 Kiton, 25 Luciano Barbera, 26 Rubinacci, 27 Silvano Lattanzi, 28 Stefano Ricci, 29 Thom Browne, 30 Tincati, 31 Aspesi, 32 No 21, 33 Re Ottavio, 34 Dolce & Gabbana, Corso Venezia, 7, 35 Dolce & Gabbana, Corso Venezia, 13, 36 Dolce & Gabbana, Corso Venezia, 15.

During the medieval period, new walls were built, and the area between the Roman walls and the medieval walls gave rise to places which were known as 'borghi', villages or hamlets. The Golden Quad fell within this area, and the borghi here were Sant'Andrea, Santo Spirito, del Gesù and Borgo Spesso, all of which live on in the names of streets in the area today.[23] It was an area which was also known for its convents and cloisters such as those which were along Via Sant'Andrea, Via del Gesù, and Via Santo Spirito. Via Borgonuovo, which today is associated with the Armani headquarters in Palazzo Orsini, was another street of convents. Milan as a city had many religious houses and the area known as the Golden Quad today was no exception. It was also conveniently near Milan's cathedral, the Duomo. Two of Milan's most exclusive hotels, The Four Seasons Hotel and the Bulgari Hotel, were also both originally convents. Via Montenapoleone was known as the Contrada di Sant'Andrea; 'contrada' was the medieval term for neighbourhood. This was where the Marliani family, supporters of the dukes of Milan, lived in Palazzo Marliani along via Montanapoleone, later used by Maria Theresa of Austria as a bank for managing public debt, and which today is home to Pasticceria Cova.[24] Also look out for the medieval arches of Porta Nuova that can still be seen along Via Manzoni just before you get to Piazza Cavour.

Of course now it's an area that's filled with international fashion houses and designer names, and which contains some of the most expensive streets in Europe, of which the most expensive is Via Montenapoleone. Life in the Golden Quad is highly competitive, with each fashion house wanting to produce the most beautiful store, and places can move around. Not everyone can actually go shopping here, but don't be put off. It's also just a lovely place to wander, breathe in the fashion atmosphere and indulge in some serious window-shopping in one of the most fascinating luxury fashion districts in the world.

Nowadays the palazzos contain luxury boutiques and flagship stores with stunning interiors designed by today's top architects, but they're also home to stories of rebels, revolutionaries, countesses and the opera world, all of which adds to the appeal. Amid the international names you'll also find 'botteghe', as they're known in Italian. These are family-run businesses that have often been passed through generations and are still producing luxury products made to the highest traditions of craftsmanship alongside museums and other places of cultural interest. There are couture houses such as Curiel, and memories of the days when Biki and Gigliola Curiel used to have breakfast together almost every week, and Gigoliola's daughter Raffaella would go with them.[25] This isn't just any luxury shopping district. This is Milan, and what makes it stand out is that Milanese filter; the beauty of its palazzos, its museums, the chic cafés and the understated feel that is so full of history and the various lives of a city through the ages. What more could any fashion lover want in life?

Put the Golden Quad right at the top of your Milanese fashion itinerary before you go. In the meantime, read on, and enter the beautiful and unique district of Milan's Golden Quad.

EAT AND DRINK

HAVING COFFEE IN one of the cafés in the Golden Quad is something you should definitely do. The cafés themselves are beautiful, and ordering an espresso at the bar, or a *caffè* as we say in Milan, amidst the smart Milanese is an experience not to be missed. But it's not only that. It's the way several worlds meet, each of which is Milan in its own unique way. It's the fashion types slouched in comfortable chairs, the informal business meeting that's going on next to you as you sip your cappuccino and eat your brioche in spite of the fact you realise it's after 11 and rather late. This is the Golden Quad just as much as it's the Milanese signora, a lady of a certain age and background, recognisable by her elegant yet understated dress, and sitting with her young grandchildren after a visit to the museum. There are two names you should know: Pasticceria Cova and Pasticceria Marchesi.

Pasticceria Cova

Cova is the legendary café and pastry shop that was opened in 1817 by Antonio Cova, a Napoleonic soldier, near La Scala opera house. It served as the headquarters for the 1848 Cinque

Pasticceria Cova

Pasticceria Cova.

Giornate (Five days of Milan) rebellion and was a meeting place for artists, intellectuals, writers, musicians and public figures including Giuseppe Verdi and Giacomo Puccini. Ernest Hemingway also used to go there and wrote about it in *A Farewell to Arms*. In 1950 it moved to Via Montenapoleone. Come here for cappuccino and brioche in the morning at the bar, or for caffè and pasticcini (espresso and exquisite mignon pastries) in the afternoon. Crystal candelabras, velvet seating, and a historic mahogany bar with marble top and brass fittings complete the atmosphere of luxury of once upon a time. Outside in the Neoclassical courtyard, designed at the end of the eighteenth century by Giuseppe Piermarini, is the Cova Garden. It was designed by architect Sonia Calzoni and inaugurated during the 2019 Design Week.

Pasticceria Cova, Via Montenapoleone, 8, 02 7600 5599, Mon–Sat 7.45 am – 8.30 pm, Sun 9.30 am – 7 pm. **www.pasticceriacova.com**

Pasticceria Marchesi

The historic pastry house Pasticceria Marchesi has been here since 2014, although Pasticceria Marchesi has been just off Corso Magenta at Via Santa Maria alla Porta 11/A since 1824. Make an experience of it, head to a table in the back room – the ones in the middle room may well be reserved – and watch how the world of the fashion crowd lounge in green velvet chairs alongside that of an older Milan that's rooted in

ritual and tradition and families that have always lived there. They also do gorgeous little boxes of sugar-coated sweets, perfect for packing in your suitcase.

Pasticceria Marchesi, Via Montenapoleone, 9, 02 7600 8238, Mon–Sun 7.30 pm – 9 pm. **www.pasticceriamarchesi.com**

LUNCH

Bice

Beatrice Mungai (Bice) was born in the cold winter of 1901 in a Tuscan village, came to Milan and opened Bice, offering Tuscan and Milanese tradition in an elegant dining room setting. Try their pappardelle al telefono: pappardelle tossed in tomato sauce and cream.

Bice, Via Borgospesso, 12, 02 7600 2572, Mon–Sun 12.30 – 2.30 pm, 7.30 – 10.30 pm. **www.bicemilano.it**

Il Salumaio di Montenapoleone

Salumaio literally means the 'person who makes the salumi' and who at one time would only sell these and a few cheeses. It opened as precisely this, along Via Montenapoleone in 1957. It's a family business that's passed from father and son for three generations and is now housed in the sixteenth-century Palazzo Bagatti Valsecchi alongside a bistro café and restaurant.

Il Salumaio di Montenapoleone, Palazzo Bagatti Valsecchi, Via Santo Spirito, 10 / Via Gesù, 5, 02 7600 1123, delicatessen Mon–Sat

8.30 am – 10.00 pm; restaurant Mon–Sat 12 – 10.30 pm; bistro café Mon–Sat 8 am – 10.30 pm. **www.ilsalumaiodimontenapoleone.it**

Panini Durini

For a nearby option that's slightly easier on your wallet, Panini Durini is a Milanese sandwich shop chain that offers good value, tasty panini and salads.

Panini Durini, Via Manzoni, 5, 02 7200 7612, Mon–Fri 7 am – 8 pm, Sat–Sun 8 am – 8 pm. **www.paninidurini.it**

APERITIVO

Bar Bulgari, Bulgari Hotel

Head to the Bulgari Hotel, owned by Bulgari (one of the world's most exclusive jewellers) and set in a renovated eighteenth-century palazzo. It's down a private street in the heart of the Golden Quad, a location that is surprisingly quiet and secluded in spite of its position, which merely adds to the exclusiveness. Bar Bulgari is the perfect place for an aperitivo. The bar's black resin oval bar counter makes a beautiful centrepiece that opens out onto the garden, at one time a monastery vegetable garden. Have lunch or dinner at Il Ristorante-Niko Romito and enjoy classic recipes and new dishes from chef Niko Romito.

Bar Bulgari, Bulgari Hotel, Via privata Fratelli Gabba, 7b, 02 805 8051, Mon–Sun 7 am – 1 am, aperitivo 6.30 – 9 pm; Il Ristorante-Niko Romito Mon–Sun lunch 12.30 – 2 pm, dinner 7.30 – 11 pm. **www.bulgarihotels.com**

Bar Martini

Bar Martini is the collaboration between Dolce & Gabbana and Martini. It was also the venue for Dolce & Gabbana's 2018 Secrets and Diamonds show that saw British millennial aristocrats and socialites wearing vintage-inspired evening wear, diamonds and tiaras to the sounds of Shirley Bassey, Marilyn Monroe and Liza Minelli. Ask for the Negroni, classic aperitivo made up of one part gin, one part red vermouth and one part Campari, and garnished with a slice of orange. The adjoining 1950s style bistrot has luscious dark red velvet and damask wallpaper, Gio Ponti-designed golden mirrors, and Italian and Sicilian dishes on the menu.

Bar Martini, Corso Venezia, 15, Bar Martini: 02 7601 1154, Mon–Sat 9.30 am – 1 am, Sun 9.30 am – 12 am.; Martini Bistrot: 02 7601 1154, Mon–Sat 12 – 3 pm, 7 pm – 12 am; Sun 12 – 3 pm, 7– 11 pm. **www.dolceandgabbana.it/ martini**

DINNER

The Manzoni by Tom Dixon

The Manzoni by Tom Dixon is British designer Tom Dixon's restaurant and showroom in Milan that opened during Design Week in 2019. Materials used were sourced from all over Italy, including marble from Verona and stone from Mount Etna, while its internal jungle has flowers from Sardinia. It's situated on the elegant

an interesting insight into a nineteenth-century Milanese home, which hosts paintings, ceramics, sculpture, lace, embroidery, jewellery, clocks and sundials and arms and armours. Poldi Pezzoli inherited the family fortune when he was only 24, and travelled and collected art as he went. The house became a living museum and is a testament to good taste of the time, and a fine example of how the Milanese who had money illustrated their lives with beautiful things in the nineteenth century. Good taste and beautiful things have always been a matter of importance to the Milanese who could afford them.

Museo Poldi Pezzoli, Via Manzoni, 12, 02 794889, 10 am – 6 pm (closed on Tuesdays). **www.museopoldipezzoli.it**

Palazzo Morando Costume Moda Immagine

Palazzo Morando, or to give it its full name Palazzo Morando Attendolo Bolognini, is where the Bolognini family lived until 1945. The palazzo was donated to the Municipality of Milan by the Countess Lydia Capraro Morando Bolognini. Nowadays, it's home to Palazzo Morando Costume Moda Immagine, Milan's fashion and costume museum, which was opened in March 2010 to showcase the collection of fabrics, clothing and accessories that make up the collections of the Museo di Milano and the Castello Sforzesco's Civic Collection of Applied Arts. The collection has around 6,000 items,

avenue named after Italian writer Alessandro Manzoni and serves up Italian and Milanese dishes.

The Manzoni by Tom Dixon, Via Alessandro Manzoni, 5, 02 8909 4348, Mon – Sat 12–3 pm, 6.30–11.30 pm, bar opens from 8.30 pm – 1am. www.**themanzoni.co**m For reservations write to reservations@themanzoni.com

CULTURE STOP

Museo Poldi Pezzoli

Museo Poldi Pezzoli was the house of art collector Gian Giacomo Poldi Pezzoli, and became a museum after his death. It's

and pieces include clothes, shoes and accessories that span from the eighteenth to the twentieth century and the years of Alta Moda. The museum provides opportunities to study fashion and costume history in all its forms, and holds temporary exhibitions, also on the theme of fashion.

The museum is also home to the Pinacoteca Luigi Beretta Collection, which charts the social and urban development of Milan during the eighteenth and nineteenth centuries through paintings, sculptures and prints showing scenes of Milan.

Palazzo Morando Costume Moda Immagine,
Via Sant'Andrea, 6, 02 8846 5735,
Tues–Sun 9 am – 1 pm, 2 – 5.30 pm.

VIA MONTENAPOLEONE

VIA MONTENAPOLEONE, known as 'Montenapo' by the locals, is Milan's most famous luxury fashion street and one of the most expensive in the world. From the medieval period and up until the eighteenth century it went by the name of Contrada di Sant'Andrea. Then Maria Theresa of Austria arrived, opened an institutional pawnbroker's and the street became Via di Monte Santa Teresa, or Contrada del Monte. Later, when Napoleon arrived, he took it over and Palazzo del Monte became the place from which Napoleon's government managed loans. Palazzo Dozio at no. 21 was the headquarters for the insurgents of the Five Days of Milan, when the Milanese rebelled against the Austrians in 1848. Carlo Cattaneo, who led the events, lived at no. 23. By the end of the nineteenth century, the area had become the heartland of the Milanese aristocracy and upper classes. Some, or rather, their descendants, do still live there, albeit far fewer than at one time.

During the first part of the twentieth century, Via Montenapoleone was the heart of a world inhabited by countesses, marchionesses, other aristocrats or distant relatives, respectable well-to-do families, and figures from the world of the nearby La Scala opera house. In the 1930s, shopping for groceries could be done at Bianchi, the baker's, and Zanocco, the 'salumeria',[26] or along Via della Spiga. It was a world where lives were passed in quiet routine. Evenings were spent in drawing rooms, trips were taken to the seaside to take in the sea air, to Liguria or Forte dei Marmi in Tuscany, or to houses on the Italian lakes. It all seems a far cry from the luxury fashion district you see today. Yet the memory remains, along with the trips to the seaside and the lakes.

Then war broke out and Milan suffered heavy bombing. Where

MARIA PEZZI

Maria Pezzi was born in Milan in 1908. Forbidden by her father to attend the city's fine arts academy, Accademia di Belle Arti di Brera, she nevertheless managed to convince him to give her permission to have private painting lessons. It stood her in good stead. In 1937 she went to Paris where she met fashion illustrator Gruau, who persuaded her to become an illustrator too. Then in 1949 she began to work for weekly news magazine *L'Europeo*, a move that launched her career in the world of journalism. Pezzi witnessed the development of fashion history first-hand. When Christian Dior launched his New Look, Pezzi was living in Paris, and her sketches were published with Elisa Massai's report of the first High Italian Fashion Show in *Women's Wear Daily*. Pezzi wrote for publications such as Il *Giorno, Donna* and *Vogue*. The pieces she wrote with her accompanying illustrations now serve as records of key moments in fashion history and have secured her place as one of the most important fashion journalists of the twentieth century.

possible, women and children were evacuated to the countryside of nearby Brianza and other places. Post-war Milan rose from the rubble and benefited enormously from the economic boom and industrial growth that followed. In a short time, Milan became a city that was favourable to growth. Stylists began to move into the street, one of which

was Mila Schön. Often referred to as the Italian Coco Chanel, she opened firstly on Via San Pietro in 1958, and then on Via Montenapoleone in 1966. Schön went into couture after her husband went bankrupt and her marriage broke down. Now no longer in a position to wear it, she decided to make it herself with the help of the seamstresses she knew. She went on to dress Jackie Kennedy and her sister Lee Radziwill, Imelda Marcos, Farah Diba, wife of the Shah of Iran, and Marella Agnelli, wife of Italian industrialist and Fiat owner Gianni Agnelli.

All this was during a time when Milanese society ladies had their clothes made by dressmakers and the couture houses of the time. When Gigliola Curiel opened her atelier just after the Second World War when she arrived in Milan from Trieste with her young daughter Raffaella, she chose a location that was nearby. The ladies of Via Montenapoleone were used to the comforts of the small area around the street where they liked to have everything they needed, including couture.[27] The Curiel atelier is now here in Via Montenapoleone, and other traces of such times remain in the historic shops along the street. Cusi jewellery opened here in the mid 1960s, although the company originally started in 1866 near the Duomo. Larusmiani, which was opened in 1922 by Giuglielmo Main who dressed stars such as Totò, Charlie Chaplin and Buster Keaton, has been on the street since 1954. Between 1939 and 1958 five Larusmiani stores were opened, including the one here on Via Montenapoleone today. The Montenapoleone store has also housed Lorenzi cutlery, another of the street's historic shops, since 2015. Bucellati and Damiani jewellers are also here, while Bulgari is the jewellers associated with film stars such as Elizabeth Taylor, Audrey Hepburn and Sophia Loren.

During the 1960s Via Montenapoleone was a street that still housed the traditional shopkeepers of the time, selling literally everything you could possibly need. It included a greengrocer's, a gentleman's tailors and an Elizabeth Arden School of Beauty. Nowadays it's a high fashion experience, where the best of international and Italian fashion names meet the best names in design and architecture, with stunning results, and remember that even along Via Montenapoleone, some addresses are more desirable than others, with the area surrounding Hermès generally viewed as the most exclusive.

Balenciaga (women's and menswear)

The interior design is in line with that of the store in Rue Saint-Honoré in Paris. Bare grey industrial-style architecture is the perfect un-intrusive backdrop with a carpet upstairs by artist Cayetano Ferrer inspired by vintage casino prints. This is the Milan flagship of iconic French fashion house Balenciaga, set up in Paris in the 1930s by Spanish-born Cristobal Balenciaga. Christian Dior considered him 'the master of us all', while Coco Chanel said Balenciaga alone was 'a couturier in the truest sense of the word…. The others are simply fashion designers.' His dresses hid feats of engineering as he experimented with abstract voluminous forms. When he died in 1972, *Women's Wear Daily* ran the headline: 'The king is dead.' Demna Gvasalia revolutionised the fashion house after he became creative director in 2015, with street style and tailoring that appeals to celebrities such as Beyoncé and Kate Moss, while some of us just swoon helplessly over sneakers, knitwear and bags.

Balenciaga, Via Montenapoleone, 23, 02 3601 8250, Mon–Sun 10 am – 7 pm.
www.balenciaga.com

Curiel (couture)

The enormous photographs in the entrance to the atelier remind you that this is one of the most important fashion houses which dressed all the society ladies at the opening night of La Scala in the post-war years when Italy, and particularly Milan, was experiencing regrowth and economic boom. It's essentially a tale of four women, and of the skill and gift of couture that has passed through their hands. Ortensia Curiel started out in her atelier in the Mitteleuropean Trieste of the early

Gigliola (centre left) and Raffaella Curiel (centre right), La Scala Opera House, 1962. Curiel

twentieth century. A cultured woman, Ortensia understood the meaning of elegance and expressed it through her couture that was appreciated in the best drawing rooms of the day. Her niece, Gigliola, then came to Milan in 1945, opened a couturier's in Via Durini and started to dress society ladies in Milan just as she had watched her aunt do in Trieste. The position of her atelier close to Via Montenapoleone, where all the well-heeled ladies lived, was wisely

chosen and her innate knowledge of how to dress women was influenced by the French haute couture shows which she attended every year. Within three years she had 128 employees. Curiel was the couture that every woman wanted, and Gigliola Curiel was the first Italian haute couturier to design exclusive collections for Bergdorf & Goodman in New York and Harrods in London in the 1950s.

Daughter Raffaella – known as Lella

– spent a year at Balmain in Paris prior to joining her mother at the atelier in 1963. Raffaella had grown up amid a world of Milanese couture. Her mother was also a friend of Milanese couturier Biki, and the two friends would have breakfast together every week, and Raffaella often went too. In 1965 she showed her first collection, and in 1969 took the helm of the atelier after her mother's untimely death. Through haute couture she was able to explore her passion for art, and her collections were inspired by artists as diverse as Dante Gabriel Rossetti, Goya and Georgia O'Keeffe. Her contribution to fashion has won prestigious awards such as The Knighthood of the Gran

The younger Gigliola Curiel at work. Curiel

Raffaella Curiel. Giovanni Gastel, courtesy of Curiel

RAFFAELLA CURIEL

'I'm very proud to create haute couture here in Milan, mostly because my mother started here in the 1950s, although I understand that is hard now. Haute couture was held in Rome in the past and is now really in mourning. Couture is experimental work, research and study, new ideas that are always copied all over the world, and mostly in ready-to-wear. Fashion history is a minor art, but it is still an art. Paris has always been the centre for couture, and we can't deny that all the best Italian couturiers go and show there. I hope my Chinese partners will decide to let Curiel show there too, although I am still very proud to show in Milan.'

Croce of the Italian Republic and the Ambrogino d'Oro of the Province of Milan. Raffaella's daughter, also named Gigliola, has worked with her mother since 1994, and in 2000 created the ready-to-wear line now known as the 'curiellino', a reference to the iconic dress that Gigliola originally gave to the Milanese ladies all those years ago.

In 2016 the fashion house began a joint venture with Chinese company Redstone. To celebrate the arrival of the company in China, Raffaella Curiel designed her September 2017 haute couture collection which she named 'Red Carpet – On the way to Shanghai.' It was dedicated to Italian opera, and opened with a spectacular, highly embroidered, red evening dress that required seventy days of work to complete. Curiel's spring/summer 2019 collection commemorated fifty years since the death of Raffaella's mother Gigliola. It was a collection that drew inspiration from the archives, and from sketches done by Gigliola over the years. A hundred years later, Curiel is still synonymous with the elegance, refinement and good taste that's not just Italian but quintessentially Milanese.

Curiel, Via Montenapoleone, 13, 02 7600 9786, Mon–Fri 9 am – 7 pm. **www.curiel.redstone**

Dior (womenswear, menswear)

The shop recalls the famous atelier at 30 Rue Montaigne with its staircase, grey walls and couture atmosphere, although couture is only sold in Paris. Maria Grazie Chiuri, Dior's only female creative director, has brought the feminist to the feminine, while making powerful statements on the catwalk. The 2020 Fall/Winter show featured powerful neon signs by feminist collective Claire Fontaine, some reading 'consent', in the week Harvey Weinstein was convicted of rape.

Dior, Via Montenapoleone, 12, 02 7631 7809, Mon–Sun 10 am – 7 pm. **www.dior.com**

Dolce & Gabbana (womenswear)

Four floors of a nineteenth-century palazzo, interiors that recreate the world of high society Milan, a touch of the baroque, high quality and precious materials, the best of Italian artisanship with Venetian stucco damask-effect walls, signature lava stone flooring, green and onyx marble, and design-piece chairs and love seat by Gio Ponti. When Dolce & Gabbana opened their first boutique here in 2016, an exclusive street party was held at the end of the September Fashion Week to celebrate. Seven tables seating sixty people and with a total length of 200 metres were set above a red carpet and adorned with flowers, fruit, candles, grapes and candelabras. It was a night to remember and to celebrate.

Domenico Dolce and Stefano Gabbana started off in Milan in 1985 when they showed their first women's collection, which was produced in Sicilian workshops. Dolce & Gabbana was mysterious, sexy and seductive. The Sicilian widow look had never been so hot. It was a heady fashion mix firmly rooted in southern Italy that mixed plates of spaghetti with those clothes and a world that evoked Rome's Cinecittà sex symbols such as Gina Lollobrigida and Sophia Loren. Exclusive Alta Moda events are attended by cherished clients wearing Dolce & Gabbana creations.

Dolce & Gabbana, Via Montenapoleone, 4, 02 7712 3711, Mon–Sun 10.00 am – 7.30 pm. **www.dolcegabbana.it**

Gucci (womenswear, menswear, childrenswear)

Gucci became the name of the day when Alessandro Michele brought it back into the limelight when he became creative director in January 2015. It's an empire that grew from the leather goods company founded in 1921 by Guccio Gucci. Gucci had worked for a while as a lift boy at the Savoy Hotel in London and went back home to Florence where he started making saddles and saddlebags. In 1938 he opened along Rome's luxury fashion street, Via Condotti, and in the 1950s and 1960s Gucci helped to bring the world of Italian accessories into the spotlight, and to become a symbol itself of luxury Made in Italy. The post-war bamboo bag of 1947 had a handle that was honed from bamboo roots, quite simply because bamboo wasn't rationed, and it became iconic, as did Gucci loafers. Tom Ford was the charismatic American who came to the helm and injected sex, glamour and 1990s androgyny through retro 1970s tailoring, white dresses that clung to the figure, and plenty of black. He tapped into the feel of the time, and his white dresses at his Fall 1996 show became legendary. Alessandro Michele has brought Gucci back into the spotlight once more with a colourful world inspired by nature, the orient, fluidity of gender and the Gucci history itself. If you're ever in Florence, head to the Gucci Garden there. The shop is on the ground floor, whereas the upper floors host the gallery with clothing from past collections and various other items that inspire Michele, and it's a fascinating insight into the world of Gucci through the years. In the meantime, come here to the flagship store on Via Montenapoleone. It was redesigned after Michele became creative director in 2015 in slightly bohemian Art Deco style, with luscious velvet upholstered cabinets and red velvet armchairs that beg to be sat in. Indulge in lavish dreams.

Gucci, Via Montenapoleone, 5/7, 02 771271, Mon–Sat 10 am – 7.30 pm, Sun 10 am – 7 pm
www.gucci.com

Gucci Garden, Piazza della Signoria, 10, Florence, 055 7592 7010, Mon – Sun 10 am – 11.00 pm (autumn/winter until 10.30 pm)
www.gucci.com

Emilio Pucci (womenswear)

Florentine aristocrat Emilio Pucci, Marquess of Barsento, became famous as the 'prince of prints'. His boutique style brought him fame at a time when the boutique look was new and distinctly Italian. Pucci was one of the major exponents of such a look, and by way of the Italian High Fashion Shows organised by Giovanni Battista Giorgini, his clothes would take it into American department stores. Pucci originally started out designing skiwear in the late 1940s, and in 1947 his streamlined ski suit appeared in *Harper's Bazaar*. He then opened a boutique on the island of Capri, specialising in so-called 'resort' clothing, which the island's exclusive clientele loved. Women adored his colourful prints, and colours such as 'Pucci pink', inspired by the bougainvillea in Capri, and 'Capri blue'. Moreover, these were clothes which gave women freedom to move, yet still retained the quality of that 'couture' look, and included easy-to-wear silk jersey dresses in joyous, colourful designs that could be packed into a suitcase. Marilyn Monroe, Lauren Bacall and Elizabeth Taylor all loved his designs, and when Monroe died tragically in 1962, she was buried in her green Pucci dress. Modern collections often draw upon prints from the archive that are revisited and refreshed for a contemporary look.

Emilio Pucci, Via Montenapoleone, 27, 02 7631 8356, Mon–Sun 10 am – 7 pm.
www.emiliopucci.it

Emilio Pucci.
BOUTIQUE EMILIO PUCCI MILANO - Via Montenapoleone, 27

KRIZIA

Mariuccia Mandelli – Krizia – was one of the first to show in Milan in the 1970s and a key figure in the rise of Made in Italy during the 1970s and 1980s. Originally an elementary school teacher from Bergamo, she went to Milan and followed her passion for clothes, and in 1954 started Krizia with her friend Flora Dolci. It was a slow beginning, with the two carrying around samples in suitcases in a Fiat 500. In 1964 Krizia showed her first collection at Palazzo Pitti, for which she received the Critico della Moda prize, the first woman to ever receive it. Krizia helped to influence the shift to Milan at the end of the 1960s. Her work was characterised by its play of contrasts, black with white, cocoon shapes, leopard and tiger print knitwear, innovative and distinct designs with their references to popular culture, which earned her the title of 'Crazy Krizia'. She's also known as the inventor of hotpants. Andy Warhol immortalised her in a series of portraits, one of which was published every day on the front page of Italian national newspaper *La Repubblica* for years, whereas Karl Lagerfeld referred to her as the 'Miuccia Prada' of the 1960s and 1970s. Krizia was a woman with her finger on the pulse of a time. Her Spazio Krizia, a theatre she opened next to the Krizia headquarters along Via Menin, was where she hosted not only fashion shows, but also cultural events with guests such as writers Doris Lessing and Arthur Miller, artists and musicians.

Krizia is now owned by Zhu Chuongyun, and reopened in premises designed by Vicenzo de Cotiis at Krizia, Via della Spiga, 23, 02 4537 7030, Mon–Sat 10 am – 7 pm. **www.krizia.it**

Prada (womenswear, menswear)

Prada's roots are Milanese and Miuccia Prada herself is Milanese. Hers is a quirky, almost awkward take on classic pieces, a vision of imperfect beauty that consistently breaks boundaries and pushes forward, while always having something that will appeal to a Milanese wardrobe. Throughout the 1970s, she was a member of the Unione Donne Italiane (Union of Italian Women) and engaged in campaigning. She received a PhD in political science and studied acting and mime at Milan's Piccolo Teatro.

She has said that when she went into the family business in 1978 she found feminism difficult to align with fashion, yet she believed that fashion was an important part of a woman's life and it was merely a question of aesthetics. Together with her husband Patrizio Bertelli, she took the luxury leather goods company that her grandfather had founded and turned it into an international success story, starting off with the now iconic nylon backpacks.

What Mrs Prada is doing is always of the highest importance, and Prada is the one everyone's eyes are on during Fashion Week. The 2012 exhibition, 'Schiaparelli and Prada: Impossible Conversations', at the Costume Institute of the New York Metropolitan Museum of Art, explored how both women challenged and deconstructed conventions of beauty and femininity, and how both had – and still have – links with the art world. Schiaparelli knew artists such as Man

Ray, Picasso, Jean Cocteau and Dali, while Prada has links with the art world most significantly through the Fondazione Prada. The tourists go to the store in the Galleria Vittorio Emanuele II. The Milanese come here to Via Montenapoleone.

Prada Women's ready-to-wear, accessories and leather goods: Via Montenapoleone, 8, 02 777 1771, Mon–Sat 10 am – 7.30 pm, Sun 10 am – 7 pm; Menswear, Via Montenapoleone, 6, 02 7602 0273, Mon–Sat 10 am – 7.30 pm, Sun 10 am – 7 pm. **www.prada.com**

Roberto Cavalli (womenswear, menswear, childrenswear)

When he was a boy, Roberto Cavalli used to walk along Via Montenapoleone, look at the luxury fashion houses and imagine that one day his own name would be up there. And so it is, above the largest Robert Cavalli boutique, complete with staircase with mother-of-pearl steps and

a 15-metre high digital videowall. There are five floors holding all the Roberto Cavalli collections, and on the second floor there's also the possibility to make an appointment for haute couture. Cavalli opened his first boutique in Saint Tropez in 1972, experimented throughout the 1970s with revolutionary techniques of printing on leather, and is famous for his iconic animal prints and use of colour.

Roberto Cavalli, Via Montenapoleone, 6/A, 02 7630771, Mon – Sat 10 am – 7.30 pm. **www.robertocavalli.com**

Salvatore Ferragamo (menswear, shoes, womenswear)

Salvatore Ferragamo was born in 1898 in Bonito, a small town 100 km away from Naples. By the age of 11, he was running his own shoemaker's and at the age of 13, he opened his own shop. A year later

Salvatore Ferragamo. Salvatore Ferragamo

Actress Joan Crawford in the Ferragamo shop, 1920s. Photo Chateau Art Studios L.A. Florence, Museo Salvatore Ferragamo

he emigrated to the United States, and in 1923 he opened the Hollywood Boot Shop, where he began what would be a long relationship with Hollywood. He made footwear, from cowboy boots to Roman sandals and Judy Garland's ruby slippers. Mary Pickford, Joan Crawford, Lauren Bacall, Ava Gardner, Greta Garbo, Anna Magnani and Marilyn Monroe all wore his shoes. On his return to Italy in 1927 he chose Florence, one of the most important Italian cities of the time, in the heartland of the Tuscan leather tradition. Ferragamo created shoes to fit the natural anatomy of the foot, and combined function with aesthetic beauty.

His iconic orthopaedic cork wedge shoes – a result of fascist nationalist economic policies and the resulting lack of materials – were revived during the 1970s. Ferragamo also experimented with other less common materials such as raffia, wood, metal, synthetic resins, and nylon thread, which resulted in his 1947 'invisible sandals'. Check out the Creations collection that draws on archive shoes and bags with its 1930s Mary Jane shoes and 1940s wedges.

Upon his death in 1960, widowed and with six children to look after, Wanda Ferragamo took the reins with her eldest daughter Fiamma, who had just turned 18, and remained as honorary chairman until her death in 2018. If you're ever in Florence, go visit the museum where exhibitions held there explore various aspects of his life and work.

Salvatore Ferragamo, womenswear: Via Montenapoleone, 3, 02 7600 0054, Mon–Sat 10 am – 7.30 pm, Sun 11 am – 7 pm; menswear: Via Montenapoleone, 20/4, 02 7600 6660, Mon–Sat 10 am – 7.30 pm, Sun 11 am – 7 pm. **www.ferragamo.com**

Salvatore Ferragamo Museum, Piazza di Santa Trinità, 5R, Mon–Sun 10 am – 7.30 pm. **www.ferragamo.com/museo**

Valentino (womenswear)

It's Valentino, king of Italian couture and creator of the famous Valentino red dresses and more. Valentino Garavani learned his trade in Paris with Guy Laroche and Jean Dessès, and then founded his fashion house in Rome in 1959 in the image of the Paris fashion houses. His debut came in 1962 at Palazzo Pitti, and then in 1967 he dedicated a series of all-white dresses known as the 'white collection' to Jackie Kennedy, whom he'd already been dressing for a couple of years by that time. It was the pivotal point in his career and gained him a place in the hearts of film-star divas. When he designed Jackie Kennedy's lace-trimmed wedding dress for her marriage to Aristotle Onassis,, he had sixty orders for the same dress the next day. Valentino was hugely instrumental in placing Italian fashion on the international stage.

In 2007 there was a spectacular exhibition of the designer's work

'Valentino a Roma: 45 Years of Style' at the Ara Pacis. The exhibition showed around 300 garments and archive materials which drew on the designer's illustrious career and emphasised his links with Rome. He gave his last ready-to-wear show in Paris in October 2008 and Pier Paolo Piccioli is now creative director. The décor here is by architect David Chipperfield, who also designed the store in Paris. It opened in February 2012 to celebrate the fashion house's 50th anniversary. At the 2019 Golden Globe Awards, all eyes were on Lady Gaga in a ravishing blue Valentino couture dress, inspired by Judy Garland's

ROME AND LA DOLCE VITA

In spite of the Italian High Fashion Shows in Florence and the couturiers working in cities such as Milan, Turin and Venice, it was Rome that held the title of capital of Italian Alta Moda, as Italian haute couture is known. Roman couture first attracted the world's attention in 1949 at the Hollywood wedding of Tyrone Power and Linda Christian. Christian was wearing a Fontana Sisters' dress which appeared on the pages of the international press. What's more, they were married in Rome, and weddings in Rome with Hollywood film stars always score high in romantic fascination and international interest. It also ensured international interest in the Roman couture house known as the Fontana Sisters, which was set up by three sisters originally from the countryside in Emilia Romagna, Zoe, Micol and Giovanna. American opera singer and actress Anna Moffo was one of the first to flock there, and she would be followed by Audrey Hepburn, Jackie Kennedy, Princess Grace of Monaco and Elizabeth Taylor. The 1949 wedding dress was a taste of what would come.

Rome in the 1950s and 60s was known as the Hollywood on the Tiber. Thanks to the city's Cinecittà and its links with Hollywood, stars of the 1950s and 1960s such as Sophia Loren and Gina Lollobrigida, it projected that Made in Italy southern Italian sexiness onto the cinema screen which would become a hallmark of the Italian dream. When Valentino opened his atelier along Via Condotti in Rome in 1959, it was within a world of film stars, royalty and fashion greats such as Coco Chanel, who stayed along the famous Via Veneto with its hotels, restaurants and bars offering their very own version of la dolce vita (literally, 'the sweet life'). It was the infinite allure of that dolce vita, of a place, its look, its food, its fashion and its parties that had such a massive appeal abroad. Tales of movie stars in Italy were reported throughout the media. There were couturiers such as the Fontana Sisters, while Sophia Loren and Gina Lollobrigida wore dresses by another couturier, Emilio Schuberth, along with other Hollywood divas and aristocrats. Films included *Roman Holiday* (1953), which showed Audrey Hepburn as a European princess riding around on a Vespa wearing Italian leisure wear, and other films such as *Three Coins in the Fountain* (1954), and *The Barefoot Contessa* (1954), for which the Fontana Sisters designed the costumes. In 1960 Anita Ekberg shot the famous Trevi Fountain scene with Marcello Mastroanni in Fellini's *La Dolce Vita*. (Much of the film was also filmed along Via Veneto.) The scene became iconic, and it was one that Valentino would recreate in his 1995 spring/summer campaign *La Dolce Vita* with Claudia Schiffer. The myth – and the marketing – of la dolce vita has always had a powerful pull.

look in the 1954 film *A Star is Born*. The look was 'old Hollywood', with matching stole, and she even dyed her hair to match the dress colour. Watch Matt Tyrnauer's *The Last Emperor* for a fascinating insight into the designer's life. REDValentino, the younger, more urban line is along Corso Venezia.

Valentino, Via Montenapoleone, 20, 02 7600 6182 Mon–Sun 10 am – 7 pm.
www.valentino.com

REDValentino, Corso Venezia, 6, 02 3675 6030, Mon–Sun 10 am – 7.30 pm.
www.redvalentino.com

Versace (womenswear, menswear)

In September 2017, twenty years after the death of her brother Gianni, Donatella Versace showed the 2018 spring/summer ready-to-wear womenswear at the Triennale Design Museum in Milan, a showcase for excellence in Italian design. 'This is a celebration of a genius,' began the voiceover. 'This is a celebration of an icon … Gianni, this is for you.' It drew on signature gold chainmail and other prints drawn from the iconic 1991–95 archives, and the grand finale opened the curtain on 1990s supermodels Naomi Campbell, Cindy Crawford, Carla Bruni, Claudia Schiffer and Helena Christensen who walked down the catwalk in gold chainmail dresses, as George Michael's 'Freedom' played on the stereo system. It was both a nostalgic and fitting celebration for a man who had brought together fashion, celebrities, and supermodels.

Gianni Versace, whose mother was a dressmaker and whose sister Donatella was his muse from a very early age, had come to Milan from Reggio Calabria. He began his career at Callaghan in 1972, opened his first shop on Via della Spiga in 1978 and went on to become the much-loved darling of Hollywood, the music world and the jet set. The choice of venue, the Triennale Design Museum, placed him in the canon of Italian fashion history with his sexy, theatrical fashion that goes against the canon of traditional Italian elegance, while maintaining the sartorial tradition. Donatella Versace took the fashion house to embrace a whole lifestyle, while maintaining a deep respect for the traditions of the family brand alongside a passion for the future.

2017 was also the year Donatella was awarded a British Fashion Award, not only for innovation, glamour and creativity, but also for the way she has shaped the fashion world and encouraged emerging designers. Other awards include the International Award at the Council of Fashion Designers of America Fashion Awards, being named Designer of the Year by *GQ UK* and *GQ China*, and the GQ Fashion Icon award, all in 2018. She also received the Green Carpet Fashion Award for her commitment to sustainable fashion in the same year, which was awarded during the September Fashion Week.

The September 2019 womenswear collection saw another iconic Versace moment when Jennifer Lopez closed the show in a revisited version of the green jungle dress which she'd worn in February 2000 to the Grammy Awards. It became the most popular item searched for on Google and led to the creation of Google Images Search.

Versace, Via Montenapoleone, 11, 02 7600 8528, Mon–Sat 10.30 am – 7.30 pm, Sun 11 am – 7 pm. www.versace.com

ALSO VISIT...

Etro started out in 1968 as a textile company and is famous for its colourful prints and paisleys. Owner Consuelo Castiglioni's daughter, Carolina Castiglioni, debuted her first collection for womenswear company Plan C in 2018. Also visit the cool white showroom of **Alberta Ferretti**, home to the trademark dresses synonymous with femininity, embroidery and detail. **Moncler** is another clothing brand that's historically popular with the Milanese. Think high-end après skiwear in ski resorts such as St Moritz and Courmayeur, which looks equally good in the city. Their Moncler Genius line involves prolific designers who design their own capsule collections, including a reinterpretation of the classic Moncler down jacket. Also check out beautiful, bohemian **Marni**, famous for its colour blocking, and located in the courtyard of a historic palazzo. **Tod's** is the popular Made in Italy leather goods company, owned by Diego della Valle. Go for beautiful, timeless bags and shoes. **Ermenegildo Zelda** started producing quality textiles in 1912 and specialises in menswear. The emphasis is on luxury with high quality materials such as linen, velvet and silk. For shoes, go to **Sergio Rossi** for Godiva pumps, heels and more at the luxury boudoir-style flagship, while **Loro Piana** specialise in luxury cashmere and the Peruvian vicuña wool that was considered the 'golden cloth' by the Incas. **Brunello Cucinelli** have also been producing luxury cashmere since they started in Solomeo, a medieval town in Umbria.

Fendi is the historic Roman fashion house that began making luxury furs and leather goods for Roman aristocratic ladies in the 1920s. Here in Milan, they're housed in a sixteenth-century Palazzo Carcassola-Grandi, complete with Agostino Bonalumi paintings and Presenze column at the entrance by the Nucleo artists' collective. The work is made from amber resin pixels in reference to the iconic sanpietrini cobblestones found in Roman streets. **Louis Vuitton** is here in the neoclassical Palazzo Taverna, with a décor designed by star architect Peter Marino, as is Yves Saint Laurent. And don't forget **Hermès**. Lose yourself amid silk scarves, Kelly and Birkin bags, and imagine you're in that convertible driving around nearby Lake Como.

Alberta Ferretti, Via Montenapoleone, 18, 02 7600 3095, Mon–Sun 10 am – 7 pm. **www.albertaferretti.com**

Brunello Cucinelli, Via Montenapoleone, 27C, 02 7601 5982, Mon–Sat 10 am – 7 pm. Sun 11 am – 7 pm. **www.brunellocucinelli.com**

Ermenegildo Zegna, Via Montenapoleone, 27/E, 02 7600 6437, Mon–Sat 10.30 am – 7.30 pm. Sunday 11 am – 7 pm. **www.zegna.it**

Etro, Via Montenapoleone, 5, 02 7600 5049, Mon–Sun 10 am – 7.30 pm. **www.etro.com**

Fendi, Via Montenapoleone, 3, 02 7602 1617, Mon–Sat 10.30 am – 7.30 pm, Sun 11 am – 7 pm. **www.fendi.com**

Loro Piana, Via Montenapoloeone, 27, 02 7772 901, Mon–Sun 10 am – 7 pm. **www.loropiana.com**

Louis Vuitton, Via Montanapoleone, 2, 02 7771 711, Mon–Sat 10 am – 7.30 pm, Sun 10.30 am – 7.30 pm. **www.louisvuitton.com**

Marni, Via Montenapoleone, 12, 02 7631 7327, Mon–Sun 10 am – 7 pm. **www.marni.com**

Moncler, Via Montenapoleone, 1, 02 7634 1316, Mon–Sat 10.30 am – 7.30 pm, Sun 11 am – 7 pm. **www.moncler.com**

JOLE VENEZIANI

Number 8, Via Montenapoleone, is where Jole Veneziani opened her atelier in 1944. As a girl from the southern Italian city of Taranto in Puglia, Veneziani had wanted to be an actress, but her mother's early death meant that she entered the fur trade. Her family moved to Milan in 1907, and in 1938 she opened a furrier's shop on Via Nerone, from where she produced furs known for their lightness and quality for the world of Alta Moda or Italian haute couture. When she moved to Via Montenapoleone in 1944, she began to create Alta Moda. Veneziani is an important name in the history of Italian fashion, who alongside her haute couture line diversified into other lines that included Veneziani Sport. She was one of the couturiers to be chosen for the first Italian fashion show, at Giorgini's Villa Torrigiani in 1951 and after the February 1952 fashion show which was reported by *Time* magazine, was awarded the Giglio d'Oro della Moda, symbol of Florence, for her contribution

to Italian Alta Moda in terms of number of sales. She was present with other important fashion names of the time in 1958 to sign the founding of the Camera Sindacale della Moda in Rome, which then became the Camera Nazionale della Moda Italiana. Over the years she welcomed many Milanese society ladies to her atelier, and stars from the world of film and opera such as Maria Callas, Josephine Baker, Marlene Dietrich, and Italian actresses Lucia Bosè and Elsa Martinelli.

Sergio Rossi, Via Montenapoleone, 27, 02 7600 6140, Mon–Sat 10 am – 7pm, Sun 11 am – 7 pm. **www.sergiorossi.com**

Tod's, Via Montenapoleone, 13, 02 7600 2423, Mon–Sat 10 am – 7.30 pm, Sun 1 pm – 7 pm. **www.tods.com**

Yves Saint Laurent, Via Montenapoleone, 8, 02 3601 9900, Mon–Sat 10 am – 7.30pm, Sun 10 am – 7 pm. **www.ysl.com**

VIA DELLA SPIGA

Via della Spiga has a history of being somewhat rebellious. During the nineteenth century, it was a popular hang-out for supporters of the 'Risorgimento' movement which worked for the unification of Italy that eventually took place in 1861 when the Kingdom of Italy was proclaimed under Vittorio Emanuele II. It was also popular with the Milanese Scapigliatura, a group of artists and intellectuals at the end of the nineteenth century, who essentially protested against the society and culture of the time, lived bohemian lives and expressed their anti-conformist values through their art.

Before the Second World War, Via della Spiga was a backstreet, with shops such as grocery stores and haberdasheries that provided the necessary services for the families who lived in the rich palazzos. After the war, it was the birthplace of another artistic movement 'Fronte nuovo delle Arti', literally, 'new face of the arts', and during the 1950s art galleries began to open along the street. Then during the 1960s the fashion boutiques began to arrive. It was significant that these weren't Alta Moda ateliers but manufactured high fashion boutiques that were inspired by the boutiques of London. Alta Moda fashion houses had been producing some ready-to-wear lines, yet these were boutiques that sold only ready-to-wear, and by designers that had a massive appeal within the youth generation of the time. Cose was opened by Nuccia Fattori in 1963, and sold clothes by Biba, Zandra Rhodes, Sonia Rikyel and Paco Rabanne, as well as collaborations with designers

Gio Moretti (womenswear, menswear)

Gio Moretti is named after owner Giovina Moretti, who opened the boutique in 1970. She brought French designers Claude Montana, Azzedine Alaïa, Thierry Mugler, Jean Paul Gaultier and Ungaro to Milan in the 1970s, and Calvin Klein and Donna Karan in the 1990s. The boutique continues to be one of the most important in Milan with three floors of fashion, including an area for books and magazines. Go there for Givenchy, Balmain, Alexander McQueen, Chloé, Versace, Giambattista Valli, Elie Saab, Zuhair Murad and more.

Gio Moretti, Via della Spiga, 4, 02 7600 3186, Mon–Sun 10 am – 7 pm
www.giomoretti.com

such as Walter Albini. Gulp was another iconic boutique of the time, which was opened on nearby Via Santo Spirito by Gabriella Barassi in 1966, as was Gio Moretti, which opened in 1970 and is still here today.

During the same period, Fiorucci opened his first boutique in Galleria Passarella in San Babila in 1967 (see page 103) and Biffi Boutique opened along Corso Genova, also during the second half of the 1960s. Roughly a decade later, in 1978, both Gianni Versace and Gianfranco Ferré opened their first boutiques here along Via della Spiga. Milan's exclusive fashion district was taking shape, and ready-to-wear Italian fashion was beginning to make its name.

Pretty Ballerinas (women's shoes)

Ballerine – or ballet pumps – are the Milanese women's footwear 'de rigeur', and not just because there are so many cobbled streets to walk over and are therefore infinitely preferable to heels. Ballerinas form part of that understated wardrobe look that carries you through from morning to evening, naturally without ever looking like you're trying too hard about it. At Pretty Ballerinas they come in all colours and styles. They also have sneakers, loafers, boots, sandals and espadrilles.

Pretty Ballerinas, Via della Spiga, 52, 02 8945 2302, Mon–Sat 10 am – 7 pm.
www.prettyballerinas.com

ALSO VISIT...
Prada have their accessories and leather goods shop along here. **Dolce & Gabbana** men's accessories and sneakers is at no. 1 and womenswear at no. 2. **Sermoneta** have been making cult leather gloves in all colours since 1960. Each pair of gloves is made to strict artisan traditions to perfectly fit the contours of the hand. **Maison Margiela** is a favourite of 10 Corso Como founder Carla Sozzani, while Nina Yashar's **Nilufar Gallery** is a must-see during Design Week.

Dolce & Gabbana, men's accessories and sneakers, Via della Spiga, 1, 02 7602 4094, Mon–Sun 10 am – 7.30 pm; womenswear, Via della Spiga, 2, 02 795 747, Mon–Sun 10 am – 7.30 pm.
www.dolcegabbana.com

Maison Margiela, Via della Spiga, 46, 02 7601 7087, Mon–Sat 10 am – 7 pm. www.**maisonmargiela.com**

Nilufar Gallery, Via della Spiga, 32, 02 02 780193, Mon 3 – 7.30 pm, Tues–Sat 10 am – 7.30 pm.
www.nilufar.com

Prada, Via della Spiga, 18, 02 780465, Mon–Sat 10 am – 7.30 pm, Sun 11 am – 7 pm. **www.prada.com**

Sermoneta, Via della Spiga, 46, 02 7631 8303, Mon–Sat 10 am – 7.30 pm, Sun 11 am – 7 pm. **www.sermonetagloves.com**

Leo Brogioni

THE ULTIMATE LUXURY SHOPPING EXPERIENCE: MELANIE PAYGE

'The most amazing thing about the Golden Quad is that we live side by side with our designers. So you might have lunch at the Four Seasons and be sitting next to Donatella Versace, or walk down the Via della Spiga and see Roberto Cavalli. Then you go to Nobu and you just run into Giorgio Armani. Dolce & Gabbana live right in the centre, there's Miuccia Prada here, and then during Design Week you come across the Missoni family. The names associated with the fashion houses are still here, that generation of designers is still around, along with the fashion families that are now in their second and third generations. There's nowhere else in the world like this, and that's what makes Milan so iconic as a fashion capital. And then there's the fact that it's all here in this concentrated fashion square. You don't have to even get in a car, you just walk out of one shop and into another, and you're offered coffee or champagne. Milan offers you the ultimate luxury shopping experience.'

Melanie Payge, personal fashion stylist, Milan
www.melaniepayge.com

VIA SANT'ANDREA

Giorgio Armani opened his first boutique here in 1983, eight years after he started his company with Sergio Galeotti. It was also here that Elvira Leonardi Bouyeure, or Biki as she was known, one of Milan's most famous couturiers between the 1940s and 1960s, had her home and atelier until her death in 1999. (Look for the commemorative plaque at number 15.) Chanel and Givenchy are also both along here. It may be difficult nowadays to talk about French fashion houses and Italian fashion houses; globalisation has changed our world so much that now it's more accurate to talk about Italian or French talents.[28] Yet certain names exude a certain charm, and Chanel and Givenchy are definitely two of these.

Like anywhere in the Golden Quad, and indeed all over Milan's historic centre, take a look at the balconies as you walk along. It's another testimony to classic Milanese style. As a Milanese friend once said to me: 'Il verde arreda,'

BIKI

Biki – or Elvira Leonardi Bouyeure – was the acquired granddaughter of Giacomo Puccini. Her maternal grandmother got married, had a daughter, and left her husband to go live with composer Giacomo Puccini, whom she later married. It was Puccini who gave Biki her nickname, Bicchi or 'biricchina' meaning rascal, the name suggested by Gabriele D'Annunzio that later would fix her place in Milanese couture. Biki mixed in circles that included the Toscanini family, dancer Isadora Duncan, the Milanese aristocratic family Visconti di Modrone, and Lucien Lelong the French couturier. Such contacts would later prove useful when she entered the world of fashion.

Biki needed to work, so she entered the fashion world with the countess Gina Cicogna. Together they presented a line of underwear that caused a stir in 1934. It was called Domina, a name given to it the Italian poet, Gabriele D'Annunzio, and it attracted an aristocratic clientele, including the last queen of Italy, Maria José of Belgium. Biki continued alone, and presented her first haute couture collection in 1936 in her atelier in Via Senato. Biki is generally remembered as the woman who dressed Maria Callas, created a diva, and through Callas helped to show Italian fashion to the world. Yet she made many other important contributions. She embraced post-war opportunities and collaborations with local textile industries, and during the boom years of the 1960s showed collections internationally in New York, Greece and Sweden. She became noted for her use of colour and was the first to notice Ottavio and Rosita Missoni, whose fabrics she began to use during the middle of the 1950s.

Rachael Martin

greenery decorates, and with the same understated class and style that you often see in the clothes of the people who live there. Milan isn't a city of multi-coloured floral balconies. Don't expect a riot of colour because you generally won't find it. Green is the background palette, with occasional touches of white, according to the canons of Milanese good taste. Even where plants are concerned, it's all about the understatement.

Armani

The Armani flagship store was along Via Montenapoleone for ten years, until Armani decided to return here to Via Sant'Andrea in 2020. Giorgio Armani opened his first boutique here in 1983, eight years after he started his company with Sergio Galeotti in 1975. This is where Armani started out, and where Giorgio Armani feels that the street has remained very much as it was during the 1970s, one of the most discreet and refined within the Golden Quad. Armani is possibly the name that's most associated with Italian fashion on an international scale. 'Re Giorgio', or 'King Giorgio' as he is known by Italians, represents Italian and in particular Milanese fashion more than any other Italian designer. It's that look of quintessential understated elegance, which is at the same time so utterly Milanese. During the 1980s Armani became famous for his suits, which softened the formality of men's suits and gave women a working wardrobe to

hold their place in any boardroom, and for the colour 'greige', that colour which lies between grey and beige. Along with the clean, tailored lines, it's a colour often associated with the Armani world which has remained a staple throughout his collections and characterises the Armani look. Nearby Palazzo Orsini in Via Borgonuovo is home to the Armani offices.

Via Sant'Andrea, 9, 02 7600 3234, Mon-Sat 10 am - 7.30 pm, Sun 11 am - 7 pm
www.armani.com

Banner (womenswear)

Banner is owned by the Biffi Boutiques Group who also have the legendary Biffi Boutiques store, which opened in the mid-Sixties along Corso Genova. Designed by architect Gae Aulenti, Banner has been open since 1993 and sells Italian and international designers including Stella McCartney, Alexander Wang, Japanese names such as Sacai, Suzusan and Junya Watanabe. Then there's JW Anderson and Stella Jean, the Haitian-Italian designer from Rome who researched the cotton industry from Benin to Brazil (and the slave trade involved) and brought all this to her September 2018 collection. Also go for La Double J dresses, Marc Jacobs, Simone Rocha, Jacquemus, Richard Quinn and Acne Studios designs and J Brand jeans. Italian fashion designer Carolina Castiglioni is here too with her brand Plan C, known for its elegant, sophisticated and

Banner. Biffi Boutiques

Biffi Boutiques

modern designs. Head to Banner during Fashion Week and you'll find all the newest talents displaying their creations here.

Banner, Via Sant'Andrea, 8/A, 02 7600 4609, Mon 10.30 am – 7.30 pm, Tues–Sat 10 am – 7.30 pm. **www.biffi.com**

Bottega Veneta (womenswear, menswear, home)

The first Bottega Veneta 'Maison' is in this beautiful eighteenth-century palazzo. It gathers all the Bottega Veneta products under one roof. There are leather goods – look out for the distinctive woven bags – luggage, shoes, men and women's ready-to-wear, fine jewellery and furniture and home collections. Creative director Daniel Lee created waves with his debut collection of September 2019 that included oversized slouchy bags in that distinct weaving.

Bottega Veneta, Via Sant'Andrea, 15, 02 7787 8115, Mon–Sun 10 am – 7 pm. **www.bottegaveneta.com**

Giambattista Valli (womenswear)

Giambattista Valli worked for Roberto Capucci in Rome where he was introduced to the world of haute couture and the expert tailoring involved before he moved to Fendi, again in Rome. He then went up to Milan to work for Krizia, and after to Ungaro in Paris where he became creative director for Ungaro Fever. In 2005 he showed his first collection in Paris, and became one of the leading lights of a new generation of designers, producing both haute couture and ready-to-wear. This is his first shop in Milan (and in Italy) in this historic palazzo along Via Sant'Andrea, designed by architect Luigi Scialanga who also designed the boutiques in Paris. The effect is that of a very elegant apartment or Valli house, as the designer refers to his boutiques, places that both reflect both the style and the culture of a place.

Giambattista Valli, Via Sant'Andrea, 12, 02 780218, Mon–Sat 10 am – 7 pm. **www.giambattistavalli.com**

Missoni (womenswear, menswear and girls)

The story of Missoni is a classic example of the Italian fashion family business, and one of the few families that are managing to keep it that way. Ottavio and Rosita Missoni met when Ottavio was an athlete at the 1948 London Olympics. They got married and started out as a textiles company in 1953 making textiles to their own design for many including Biki, and still produce textiles for the main fashion lines today. Missoni literally updated knitwear and took it into new realms. Their revolutionary industrially produced knitwear is famous for its patterns of stripes and zigzags, and colour. It created the distinctive Missoni style that every woman wanted to wear and that still makes it so recognisable today. It was comfortable and ready-to-wear, and just like Emilio Pucci's prints in the 1950s, it could all be packed into a suitcase. 1967 saw the company's first fashion show at the prestigious Palazzo Pitti in Florence, although events didn't go quite as planned. The models' underwear was too evident so Rosita Missoni asked them to take it off, and the result left very little to the imagination. They may not have been invited back the following year, but the fashion world took note, especially influential Italian fashion journalist Anna Piaggi. The Missoni family business has become one of the most iconic brands in Italian fashion, and the family tradition continues and thrives. The company has been under the artistic direction of daughter Angela since 1997, while her daughter Margherita is creative director of the company's M Missoni brand. Go take a look at the iconic stripes and patterns of Missoni style, all in twenty-first century key.

Missoni, via Sant'Andrea on the corner of Via Bagutta, 02 7600 3555, Mon–Sat 10 am – 7.30 pm, Sun 11 am – 7 pm.
www.missoni.com

Miu Miu (womenswear)

Founded in 1993, Miu Miu is named after Miuccia Prada's nickname. Go for unexpected contrasts, surprising combinations of colour and fabric, attention to detail in buttons and jewel appliqués, beautifully soft handbags and the most exquisite feminine heels.

Miu Miu, Via Sant'Andrea, 21, 02 7600 1799, Mon–Sat 10.30 am – 7.30 pm, Sun 11am – 7 pm.
www.miumiu.com

Moschino (womenswear, menswear, childrenswear)

Franco Moschino was the designer who started producing fashion that was innovative and often a parody of fashion itself. He was originally inspired by Jean Paul Gaultier, then found his own ground by fusing popular culture with his own sense of irony to make provocative statements about the fashion system as a whole, while climbing to its echelons. Nearly twenty years after Franco Moschino's death in 1994, Jeremy Scott took over creative direction of the company. Scott believed he was the only person around who would be able to take over Moschino and understand its rebellious anti-fashion manifesto that continues today. This Milan flagship store gathers it all together under one roof. There's couture, Boutique Moschino, menswear, Baby Kid and Teen, jewellery, perfume and eyewear, all in an almost surreal white space with giant mannequins and iconic Moschino fashion pieces.

Moschino, Via Sant'Andrea, 25, 02 7602 2639, Mon–Sat 10 am – 7 pm, Sun 11 am – 7 pm.
www.moschino.com

ALSO VISIT...
The **Givenchy** flagship store was given a new look when Clare Waight Keller became creative director at the legendary French fashion house founded by Hubert de Givenchy, icon of Parisian chic. The interiors are a throwback to details from the original premises at Avenue George V in Paris, with herringbone parquet and mirrors. For more Parisian chic, head to **Chanel**, and to **Roger Vivier**, the designer of both stiletto heels and the Pilgrim pumps with silver buckles that were famously worn by Catherine Deneuve in the 1960s film *Belle du Jour*. Marlene Dietrich, Josephine Baker and Jeanne Moureau also wore his shoes, along with Queen Elizabeth II on her coronation. **Cesare Paciotti** mixes artisan tradition with high quality materials and dresses the feet of celebrities such as Rihanna, Beyoncé and Kim Kardashian. **Casadei** is also here.

Casadei, Via Sant'Andrea, 1, 02 7600 1164, Mon–Sat 10 am – 7pm. **www.casadei.com**

Cesare Paciotti, Via Sant'Andrea, 8, 02 7600 1338, Mon–Sat 10 am – 7 pm, Sun 11 am – 7 pm. **www.cesare-paciotti.com**

Chanel, Via Sant'Andrea, 10/A, 02 7788 6999, Mon-Sat 10 am – 7 pm. **www.chanel.com**

Givenchy, Via Sant'Andrea, 11, 02 7862 3710, Mon–Sat 10 am – 7 pm, Sun 11 am – 7 pm. **www.givenchy.com**

Roger Vivier, Via Sant'Andrea, 17, 02 7602 5614, Mon–Sat 10 am – 7pm, Sun 11 am – 7 pm. **www.rogervivier.com**

VIA GESÙ

Gianni Versace lived here in his Milanese apartment, Palazzo Versace, where he had his atelier and offices and a steady stream of visitors from the film and music world, and still today it's a focus for parties during Fashion Week. In January 2015 Via Gesù was inaugurated as 'la via dell'uomo', literally, 'the man's street'. It is Milan's first street that is dedicated entirely to menswear and men's lifestyle. It's also been called Milan's equivalent of London's Savile Row, and is a showcase for some of the most important and prestigious names in the history of Italian menswear and tailoring. Tailor's **Rubinacci**

has its own 'men only' club room. Gennaro Rubinacci was a tailor from Naples who started selling men's clothes under the brand London House (after the tailors of Savile Row), which were a lighter version suitable for southern climates. **Brioni** was the first Italian tailor to hold a men's catwalk show in 1952 using male models, and to promote industrially produced Made in Italy. Then in 1982 it opened its first tailoring school to continue what is known as the Brioni sartorial method.

Kiton, **Stefano Ricci**, **Barba Napoli** and **Luciano Barbera** all have shops here. For shoes, there's New York based **Thom Browne**, **Silvano Lattanzi** for handmade shoes, **Doucal's**, **Tincati** for classic Milanese tailoring, and **Doriani** for cashmere.

Complete the gentleman's experience by staying at the five star **Four Seasons Hotel** housed in a fifteenth-century convent, one of Milan's most prestigious hotels and always at the centre of Fashion Weeks. This is where Anna Wintour stays, and where Karl Lagerfeld used to stay when he was in town. The hotel has an interesting history. When the building was being converted into the hotel in the 1980s, the story emerged of an old convent and cloister, the traces of which had been hidden when it was turned into a private residence in the eighteenth century. As the builders undertook the conversion of the building into a hotel, Renaissance columns appeared. Frescoes and stuccos followed, some of which were dated as belonging to the medieval period. Everything was carefully restored, and today it's all part of the unique stay that the Four Seasons offers to its guests.

It's also a perfect example of how fashion lives alongside a far older world in the Golden Quad, a world of monasteries, convents, religion and power that played such an important role during medieval times. And it's all right here, and naturally just a stone's throw from the Duomo.

Barba Napoli, Via Gesù, 19, 02 7628 0782, Mon – Sat 10 am –7 pm, Sun 11 am – 7 pm. **www.barbanapoli.com**

Brioni, Via Gesù, 2, 02 7639 0086, Mon–Sat 10 am – 7 pm, Sun 11 am – 7 pm. **www.brioni.com**

Doucal's, Via Gesù, 15, 02 7601 3732, Mon–Sat 10 am – 7 pm. **www.doucals.com**

Kiton, Via Gesù, 11, 02 7639 0240, Mon–Sat 10 am – 7 pm. **www.kiton.it**

Luciano Barbera, Via Gesù, 9, 02 3673 7676, Mon–Sat 10 am – 7 pm. **www.lucianobarbera.it**

Rubinacci, Via Gesù, 1, 02 7600 1564, Mon–Sat 10 am – 7 pm. **www.marianorubinacci.net**

Silvano Lattanzi, Via Gesù, 11, 02 7602 8499, Mon 3 – 7 pm, Tues–Sat 10 am – 7 pm. **www.silvanolattanzi.it**

Stefano Ricci, Via Gesù, 3, 02 798588, Mon–Sat 10 am – 7 pm, Sun 3 – 7 pm. **www.stefanoricci.com**

Thom Browne, Via Gesù, 10, 02 7600 7467, Mon–Sat 11 am – 7 pm, Sun 12 – 7 pm. **www.thombrowne.com**

Tincati, Via Gesù, 7, 02 7602 8050, Mon–Sat 10 am – 7 pm. **www.tincatimilano.it**

CORSO VENEZIA, Via MANZONI AND OTHER ADDRESSES

Corso Venezia and Via Manzoni are two elegant avenues with some of Milan's most beautiful Neoclassical palazzos, such as Palazzo Serbelloni where Napoleon stayed with his wife Joséphine de Beauharnais, empress and fashion icon who inspired many a European court; and the Villa Reale, which is now the city's modern art gallery. Via Manzoni, considered one of Europe's most luxurious avenues of the nineteenth century, is full of luxury boutiques and showrooms. Look out for the elegant Grand Hotel et de Milan where composer Giuseppe Verdi used to stay in suite 501, and where he died in 1901. Via Bigli, 21, is where the countess Clara Maffei lived, and where she received writers, artists and musicians during the Risorgimento, the period during which Italy was unified. Corso Venezia leads towards the Porta Venezia area, which is covered in a separate chapter.

Take a walk along Via Borgospesso. This is where Germana Marucelli opened her first atelier in 1938 when she came to Milan. She was only there for a short time as the outbreak of war forced her to abandon it and move to Stresa. She came back after the war, and in 1949 took over the premises of fashion house Ventura on Corso Venezia. Marucelli anticipated Christian Dior's New Look with its cinched waists and full skirts, and took part in the First Italian High Fashion Show at Giorgini's home in Florence. (see page 17)

ARMANI / MANZONI 31 – EMPORIO ARMANI CAFFÈ' AND RISTORANTE – NOBU MILANO AND ARMANI HOTEL MILANO

The Armani Store opened here in 2000 to celebrate twenty-five years in the fashion industry of the designer who is possibly most associated with elegance, simplicity and that which is exquisitely beautiful. The 1935 building in which the store is housed is an impressive example of Rationalist architecture. It gathers Emporio Armani, EA7, perfumes, skincare and make-up, Armani/Fiori (a florist), Armani/Libri, a well-stocked bookshop with fashion and design titles, Armani/Dolci chocolatier's and more all under one roof. Join the fashion crowd for cocktails sitting on the 7th floor at the Armani/Bamboo Bar and try its first Capsule Collection of Signature Cocktails, a tribute to the world of Armani in its manifold creative expressions. Enjoy 'Il Re' dedicated to Giorgio Armani, elegant and precious, garnished with a golden leaf, balanced and with a sophisticated taste. It's created with gin or vodka, saffron-infused vermouth and golden leaf. Or try the 'Made to Measure' cocktail, which derives from the idea of engaging in a personalised and tailored experience, just like a skilled tailor who creates clothes with passion and care. It's created with sugar syrup, fennel liqueur, red fruit infusion and a finish of feminine or masculine perfume to be chosen by the client.

The Emporio Armani Caffè and Ristorante offers Milanese and Italian culinary tradition, while Nobu cooks up Japanese with Peruvian and Italian influences and hosts all the biggest parties during Fashion Week. The first Armani hotel opened in 2010 in Dubai, and in 2011 it was followed by the one in Milan. The hotel here has ninety-five exquisite rooms and suites, all with the sleek lines and elegance of the Armani brand.

Armani/ Manzoni 31, Via Manzoni, 31, 02 7231 8600, Mon-Sat 10 am – 8 pm, Sun 10.30 am – 7.30 pm.

Armani Bamboo Bar, Via Manzoni, 31, 02 8883 8888, Mon–Sat: 10.30am – 1am, Sun 11 am – 1 am.

Emporio Armani Caffè, Via Croce Rossa, 2, 02 62312680, Mon–Sun 9 am – 8 pm.

Emporio Armani Ristorante, Via dei Giardini, 2, 02 62312680, Mon–Sat 12.30 – 2.30 pm, 7.30 – 10.30 pm, Sun 12.30 – 9 pm.

Nobu, Via Pisoni, 1, 02 6231 2645, Restaurant Mon-Sat 12.30 – 2.30 pm, 7.30 – 11 pm, Sun 7.30 – 11 pm, Bar Mon-Sat 12:30 – 3 pm, 7 – 11.30 pm, Sun 7 – 11.30 pm.

Armani Hotel Milano, Via Manzoni, 31, 02 8883 8888
www.armani.com

Aspesi (womenswear, menswear)

Renowned for its use of unusual fabrics, Aspesi is a favourite with the Milanese for its down jackets, windbreakers, well-cut trousers and slogan t-shirts. The company was started in Legnano in the northwestern part of Milan by Alberto Aspesi in 1969 and made the beautifully cut women's and men's shirts that today are still a staple in any self-respecting Milanese wardrobe. Their flagship store changed premises and moved here in 2019, where space is also given for emerging artists to display their work. Lorenzo Vitturi created the art installation 'Retouches', made with Aspesi materials, to mark the store's inauguration.

Aspesi, Via San Pietro all'Orto, 24, 02 7602 2478, Mon–Sun 10 am – 7 pm.
www.aspesi.com

Dolce & Gabbana

Dolce & Gabbana have three shops along Corso Venezia. No. 7 is for men, women and children, no. 13 for men's tailoring and no. 15 for menswear with a barber's and men's grooming salon. There's also a men's only shoemaker's with polished parquet flooring and Gio Ponti and Franco Albini design pieces.

Dolce & Gabbana, menswear, womenswear and childrenswear, Corso Venezia, 7, 02 7600 4091, Mon–Sun 10 am – 7.30 pm; menswear boutique, Corso Venezia, 15, 02 7602 8485, Mon – Sun 10.30 am – 7.30 pm.
www.dolcegabbana.com

No 21 (womenswear, menswear)

Visit the Milan flagship store of Alessandro Dell'Acqua's brand, renowned for its knits and statement t-shirts. The store is a minimalist space designed by architect Hannes Peer. It pays tribute to Milanese architecture through its use of Ceppo di Gré, a typical stone from Romanesque architecture that's also used in the Duomo and in the columns of the Basilica di Sant'Ambrogio, Dell'Acqua's own personal tribute to Milan.

No 21, Via Santo Spirito, 14, 02 781957, Mon–Sat 10 am – 7 pm. **www.numeroventuno.com**

Re Ottavio (haute couture accessories)

Re Ottavio is a 'bottega storica', one of Milan's historical shops that conserves artisan traditions. It's a family business that was started by Sergio Coletto's father in 1934. They still make buttons, handmade and covered with fabric, pearls, Swarovski and other decorations for garments from daywear through to evening wear. They also create belts, buckles, bijoux and other accessories and have vintage costume jewellery from the 1940s and 1950s which has formed part of various exhibitions, and original buttons

GERMANA MARUCELLI

Germana Marucelli was another important couture name, and greatly significant in the development of Italian couture as opposed to the predominance of French couture and French-couture models which had dominated for so long. Born in 1905 in Settignano, near Florence, she became an apprentice at the dressmaker's belonging to her aunt and uncle at the age of 11. Her first trip to Paris was with her aunt in 1921. At the time Paris was the source of inspiration for Italian couturiers and dressmakers and dress design models were sold to be copied by 'modelliste', as they were known.

In 1932 Marucelli moved to Genoa, and in 1938 to Milan, where her generous client Flora d'Elys gave her both a home and an atelier in an apartment on Via Borgospesso. Marucelli was famous for her ability to copy French models down to the minutest detail. After the war, in 1946 she was one of the only dressmakers not to go to Paris, a decision made by choice, but also by necessity. Her designs

anticipated Christian Dior's New Look and on a personal level, this convinced her that she didn't need Paris, and gave her the confidence to follow her instincts. In 1950 Marucelli took over the exclusive Ventura atelier in Corso Venezia 18, and in 1951 she took part in the first Italian High Fashion Show organised by Giovanni Battista Giorgini.

Marucelli is considered to be one of Italy's most important stylists after the war, and lived in a world where she surrounded herself with the best of the Milanese intellectual élite and in doing so brought their world and the world of fashion together. The Thursday afternoons that she held in her atelier on Corso Venezia were considered Milan's 'salotto culturale' or cultural drawing room, where writers, artists, poets and journalists gathered, and in 1947 she founded the Premio San Babila, a poetry prize. Marucelli left the fashion world in 1972 during the advent of ready-to-wear, preferring to concentrate only on a few treasured clients and on a sewing school that was limited to close circles and family.

from the 1940s to the 1980s. The creations here are as exquisite as you would expect for clients that include designers from the world of Italian haute couture.

Re Ottavio, Via Bagutta, 1, 02 7600 2569, Mon–Fri 8.30 am – 12.30 pm,
2.30 – 5.30 pm.
www.re-accessorimoda.it

ALSO VISIT...
The bohemian, slightly retro clothes at Florentine company **Ottod'Ame** may well make you want to dress up and go laze around 1930s Villa Necchi Campiglio. **DAAD Dantone** sources all the best alternative men's and women's fashion names and places them all under one

THE FASHION LOVER'S LIST: OUTLETS

The outlets are often the saving grace of any fashion lover's wardrobe, and luckily Milan has its fair share. If you're here during the sales, discounted goods can plummet to up to 80% of the original price.

1. DMAG Designer Outlet (menswear, womenswear, childrenswear)
DMAG has three shops. It stocks a wide range including Prada, Miu Miu, Dolce & Gabbana, Gucci, Ann Demeulemeester and Comme des Garçons. Discounts are from 50% to 70% of the original retail price of clothes and shoes by the most important Italian and international designers. Look out for end of January sales when discounts go up to 80%. Via Manzoni, 44, 02 3651 4365, Mon–Sun 10 am – 7.30 pm; Via Bigli, 4, 02 3664 3888, Mon–Sun 10 am – 7.30 pm; Via Forcella, 13, 02 3676 8580, Mon–Sat 10.30 am – 7 pm. Via Manzoni and Via Bigli stores are both central in the Golden Quad. The Via Forcella store is in Zona Tortona. www.dmag.eu

2. DT Intrend Go for Maxmara, Max & Co and their own DT Intrend label just off Corso Vittorio Emanuele II. DT Intrend, Galleria San Carlo, 6, 02 7600 0829, Mon–Sun 10 am – 8 pm. www.diffusionetessile.com

3. Etro outlet Womenswear, menswear and textiles for the home, all by Etro. The outlet is based in the south of Milan, near where the company was founded in 1968. To get there you need to take a number 9 tram, get off at Viale Monte Nero and walk to Via Spartaco. Via Spartaco, 3, 02 5502 0218, Mon to Sun 10 am – 7 pm. www.etro.com

4. Il Salvagente Il Salvagente is a Milanese institution, Milan's first fashion outlet which opened on Via Bronzetti in 1978. Go for high-end fashion including Prada, Armani, Chloé, Balenciaga, Alberta Ferretti and many more. Via F.lli Bronzetti, 16, 02 7611 0328, Mon 3 pm–7.30 pm, Tues to Sat 10 am – 7.30 pm, Sun 11 am – 2 pm, 3–7 pm.
www.salvagente.com (See their website for details of how to get there.)

5. The Highline Outlet Placed right in the centre along Corso Vittorio Emanuele II, this is one of Milan's biggest outlets with a huge range of men's, women's and children's discounted clothing, shoes and accessories at up to 70% discount with lots of big designer names. Corso Vittorio Emanuele II, 30, 02 7601 4870, Mon–Fri 11 am – 8 pm, Sun 10 am – 8.30 pm. www.thehighlineoutlet.eu

6. Valextra Factory Store (leather goods)
A short walk from the centre, the Valextra outlet offers bags at discounts of between 30% and 70%. Via Cerva, 11, 02 7600 3459, Mon–Sat 10 am – 7 pm.
www.valextra.com

roof. **Valextra** began its life in Piazza San Babila in 1937 under the direction of Giovanni Fontana, who designed exotic luggage for the international jet set. Princess Grace of Monaco, Maria Callas, Jackie Kennedy Onassis and her husband and Aristotle Onassis were all clients. **Gianvito Rossi** (son of Sergio Rossi) is also along here for feminine shoes. For luxury homeware and furnishings, head to **Armani/Casa**.

Armani/Casa Milano, Corso Venezia, 14, 02 7626 0230, Mon–Sat 10.30 am – 7.30 pm. **www.armani.com**

DAAD Dantone, Via Santo Spirito, 24A, 02 7601, Mon 2–7.30 pm, Tues–Sat 10 am – 7.30 pm. **www.daad-dantone.com**

Gianvito Rossi, Via Santo Spirito, 7, 02 7628 0988, Mon 10.30 am – 7.30 pm, Tues–Sat 10 am – 7.30 pm. **www.gianvitorossi.com**

Ottod'Ame, Via Manzoni, 39, 02 6556 0409, Mon–Sat 10 am – 7.30 pm, Sun 11.30 am – 7 pm. **www.ottodame.it**

Valextra, Via Manzoni, 3, 02 9978 6060, Mon–Sat 10 am – 7 pm, Sun 11 am – 7 pm. **www.valextra.it**

MILANESE STYLE, A QUESTION OF BEAUTY

They say that Milan is 'modaiola', or fashionable. Milan as a city loves fashion. Its people work in fashion, and ask anyone in Milan and chances are they'll know someone who's involved in fashion at some level. The Milanese have a love of fashion that's present in every part of their lives, whether it's the clothes they wear, their homes, the bars they go to or the shops they love. Take a walk down the city streets and you'll see this sense of fashion, from young teenagers just out of school at lunchtime, to women going about their business. It's a love of beautiful things. This question of beauty, that which is beautiful, is at the basis of Italian fashion, and finds its expression in the city's artisan workshops and ateliers through quality materials and craftsmanship. What marks Milan out is that the Milanese concept of 'beautiful' is refined and simple. Beauty is a question of good taste, is never showy and generally always understated. It's the ability to own luxury without it becoming vulgar, being able to carry off such elegance and style without it ever appearing crass, and applying this to every area of your life.

BRERA
Boutiques, vintage shopping and art galleries

M2 Lanza, M3 Montenapoleone

During the middle of the last century, there was a place called Brera and a bar called Bar Jamaica. Brera was bohemian, anti-conformist, and a favourite haunt of the artists, writers and theatre people that made up the cultural and artistic world of 1950s and 1960s Milan. It was a place where people met for discussion, popular with artists and intellectuals and a district that was still inexpensive enough for them to live in and feed themselves on a dish of minestrone at Bar

Santa Maria del Carmine Church in Brera.

BRERA.
1 Antonia
2 Cavalli e Nastri
3 Demaldè
4 Glamour in Rose
5 L'Autre Chose
6 Luisa Beccaria
7 Madame Pauline
8 Slam Jam
9 Vintage Delirium by Franco Jacassi
10 Giolina e Angelo
11 Goods
12 L'Artigiano di Brera
13 La Tenda
14 Le Solferine
15 Ottico Marchesi

Jamaica or a dish of cotecchino and lentils at trattorias such as the Sorelle Pirovano because it was cheap and it filled you up. Bar Jamaica was frequented by artists such as Lucio Fontana, Piero Manzoni and Emilio Tadini. Allen Ginsberg came here, Salvatore Quasimodo used to come here, the Sicilian poet and novelist who won the Nobel Prize in Literature in 1959. Photographer Ugo Mulas took his earliest photos here when someone first put a camera in his hands. He was given a few basic instructions, and that was that. Like many photographers of the time, Mulas earned his living with fashion and advertising photography. He went on to become one of the greatest Italian photographers, most

Anna Piaggi.

to the fashion magazines. Piaggi in her turn would take her intellectual and cultural world to the world of fashion, and particularly to her cult *Vogue* series, 'Doppie Pagine' (double pages), which ran for twenty-four years. The 'Doppie Pagine' placed fashion within a larger context of the arts and mixed text with graphics to create her own fashion language in her own unique space. In 1962 they got married in New York, and worked together until Castaldi died in the 1990s, having become one of the most important Italian fashion photographers. Piaggi was the antithesis of Milanese understatement with her own extravagant, theatrical way of dressing, a living canvas in constant evolution. She loved vintage clothing before it became a thing, and was guided by antique clothing dealer Vernon Lambert, whom she met in 1967 in the swinging London of the time to which she was so attracted. Lambert was already selling vintage to wealthy clients in London, and together they went all over, looking for finds. Piaggi's legacy within the fashion world is great. She was one of the first to take note of Missoni when they were starting out. Karl Lagerfeld referred to her many times as his muse, as did Stephen Jones, who made many hats for her, and Manolo Blahnik. Lagerfeld once wrote that Piaggi 'invents' fashion. He fully understood her use of fashion as a form of performance art, and sketched her more than 200 times. (His drawings

notably for his street photography and portraits of artists.

Fashion journalist Anna Piaggi (pictured above) also used to frequent Bar Jamaica, as did fashion photographer Alfa Castaldi. At the time, Piaggi was working as a translator for Mondadori, and Castaldi introduced her

are gathered in Lagerfeld's *Sketchbook: Karl Lagerfeld's Illustrated Fashion Journal of Anna Piaggi*.) Piaggi, with her unique dress sense and electric blue hair, was the fashion journalist who stood out from the rest. She was loved by many, and had a wardrobe that read like a history of fashion itself. Manolo Blahnik called her the world's last great authority on frocks.

Bar Jamaica is still here today, although come now and you'll mingle with the tourists who are sitting at the tables in the street. Nowadays Brera is more a mix of high-end boutiques, jewellers, antiques and design shops in one of Milan's loveliest contexts, with its restaurants and bars and tables outside along cobbled streets. The Brera Design District is one of Milan's most important locations during the Fuorisalone programme of Milan's Design Week. (Fuori salone literally means 'outside the salone'; the Salone Internazionale del Mobile is the international furniture fair main event.) Fashion and design come together, and the district's galleries and boutiques host design events. Brera is also home to some of Milan's best vintage shops, perfect if your grandmother doesn't happen to have that vintage Gucci handbag, and if you've never heard of Pirovano or Roberta di Camerino bags, now is your time to learn.

Above all, Brera is famous for its artistic tradition. It's home to the Pinacoteca di Brera, one of Italy's most important art collections, and the Accademia di Belle Arti di Brera, Milan's fine arts' academy, both of which were established during the Austrian rule of the eighteenth century. Maria Theresa of Austria played a huge role in the area's development. She made the Palazzo di Brera the city's cultural centre, which included the Brera Astronomical Observatory, the Biblioteca Nazionale Braidense, and the adjoining botanical garden. Fernanda Wittgens, first female director of the Pinacoteca and the first to hold such a role in Italy, was the Pinacoteca's director during the Second World War. She saved the museum's collection from both the bombings and the Nazis, just before the Pinacoteca was hit in August 1943. When she came out of prison in 1945 after being sent there for helping Jews to escape, she brought the museum back to life and was the first to hold fashion shows in the gallery.

The gallery and the fine arts' academy have obviously influenced the development of the area. Artists began to frequent the area towards the end of the nineteenth century, and during the 1920s private art galleries began to open. Cesare Crespi has been open since 1880, and has been selling art supplies to Milanese artists and many others since then. He's next to where architect Gae Aulenti lived. Also take a walk along Via Ciovasso with its art galleries. It's deceptively unassuming, one of those narrow streets with the cobbled paving, shades-of-ochre buildings and wrought iron balconies with trailing greenery that are so characteristic of Brera. That's the beauty of Brera, quiet streets that feel hidden away, and right in the centre of Milan.

Bar Jamaica, Via Brera, 32, 02 876723, 9 am – 2 am every day. **www.jamaicabar.it**

Cesare Crespi, Via Brera, 28A, 02 862893, Mon–Fri 9am – 7.30 pm, Sat 9am – 1pm, 2.30 – 7.30 pm. **www.crespi-brera.com**

EAT AND DRINK

COFFEE

Caffè Fernanda Named after director Fernanda Wittgens, this 1950s inspired café has walls of the same blue that you can find in the gallery, a beautiful walnut and brass bar, paintings on the wall by Pietro Dalmini and Bertel Thorvaldsen, and a bust of Wittgens by Marino Marini. It's open to the general public, so you don't necessarily have to go into the Pinacoteca to go there, although I thoroughly recommend you do if you have time.

Caffè Fernanda, Via Brera, 28, 02 7226 3264, Tues–Sun 8.30 am – 7.15 pm (open till 10.15 pm every third Thursday of the month).

LUNCH OR DINNER

Drogheria Milanese Head to Drogheria Milanese for tapas-style dishes, pasta and burgers.

Rachael Martin

Via San Marco, 29, 02 4548 8837, Mon-Sun 12–3 pm, 7 pm – 12 am. **www.drogheriamilanesi.it**

APERITIVO

N'Ombra de Vin What used to be a refectory for Augustine friars is now a bohemian style wine bar with a menu of salads, carpaccio and fish.

N'Ombra de Vin, Via San Marco, 2, 02 659 9650, Mon – Sun 10 am – 2 am. **www.nombradevin.it**

CULTURE STOP

Pinacoteca di Brera The Pinacoteca is one of Italy's most prestigious museums with its collections of Lombard, Venetian and Emilian art. There are works by Bellini, Mantegna, Piero della Francesca, Raffaello, Rubens, Veronese, Tiziano and Caravaggio, and Francesco Hayez's famous painting *Il Bacio* (The Kiss). Look out for the painting know as the *Pala Sforzesca,* which shows Beatrice d'Este and Ludovico Sforza.

Pinacoteca di Brera, Via Brera, 28, 02 7726 3264, Tues–Sun 8.30 am – 7.15 pm (open until 10.15 pm every third Thursday of the month). **www.pinacoteca.org**

Orto Botanico

The botanical garden that adjoins the Pinacoteca was built upon the wishes of Maria Theresa of Austria in 1774 and is a must-visit during Design Week.

Orto Botanico, Via Brera, 28, 02 5031 4683, April-October 10 am – 6 pm, November–March Mon–Sat 9.30 am – 4.30 pm. Open first Sunday of every month, excluding festival days. **www.museoortibotanicistatale.it**

SHOPPING

Antonia (womenswear, menswear)

Antonia Giacinti started as a shop assistant and worked her way up to the top. Her showcase for international designers in Brera broke all the rules when it opened in 1999, both with the shop's groundbreaking design by architect Vincenzo de Cotiis, and with what she sold. It's at the forefront of the Milan

boutique scene and sells a range of labels that includes Gucci, Fendi, Givenchy, Balenciaga, Acne Studios, Isabel Marant and The Row. Menswear includes Heron Preston, Paul & Shark, Amiri, Alanui knitwear, and Palm Angels, Francesco Ragazzi's take on the Californian skater look, inspired by Manhattan Beach and Venice Beach. The shop is in the beautiful Palazzo Cagnola, which was built in 1824.

Antonia, Via Cusani, 5, 02 8699 8340, Mon 3–7.30 pm, Tues–Sat 10 am – 7.30 pm. **www.antonia.it**

Cavalli e Nastri (vintage womenswear and menswear)

Cavalli e Nastri was founded by Claudia Jesi at the end of the 1980s and has three shops in Milan. The shop in Via Brera sells partly 1990s designer clothing, and partly vintage pieces dating from the 1950s, but

Cavalli e Nastri

Cavalli e Nastri. Cavalli e Nastri

only if an item has a certain charm or if it has played some part in fashion history. The selection includes mid-century cocktail dresses including Biki and luxury handbags, also by Italian names such as Pirovano and Roberta di Camerino. There's a lot to admire, including Chanel bijoux, 1950s Borsalino hats, Hermès scarves and 1970s handbags. A dressmaking service is offered, so if a client likes a particular vintage piece, it can be made up in their size, and in a month or so you can walk out in your own version of that 1950s cocktail dress you fell in love with. They

also have their own range that takes its inspiration from vintage textiles and silhouettes. Also visit their shops on Via Gian Giacamo Mora, just off Corso di Porta Ticinese (see page 166).

Cavalli e Nastri, Via Brera, 2, 02 7200 0449, Mon–Sat 10.30 am – 7.30 pm, Sun 12–7.30 pm. **www. cavallienastri.com**

Demaldè (vintage and antique jewellery and bijoux)

Owners Elvio and Loredana are specialists in vintage and antique bijoux and costume jewellery. They create their own pieces, and stock bracelets, rings, earrings, brooches and cufflinks which cover the whole of the twentieth century. They're most famous for their range of cufflinks, which come in gold, silver and metal and include classic designs, along with more fun ones such as Vespas and guitars, and 1950s American models. The shop is small, along one of Milan's loveliest streets, and that all adds to its attraction. Walk in and you're surrounded by a treasure trove of curiosities and beautiful items. Their pieces are often used for fashion shoots, TV shows, in films, and by theatres such as La Scala and Piccolo Teatro. In 2019 they designed earrings for Antonio Marras' collection during Fashion Week.

Demaldè, Via Ponte Vetero, 22, 02 8646 0428, Mon 3.30–7.30 pm, Tues to Sat 10.30 am – 7.30 pm. **www.demaldemilano.com**

Glamour in Rose (womenswear)

Glamour in Rose specialise in evening dresses in winter and boho chic and beachwear in summer with bikinis and beachwear. The boutique started in the seaside resort of Forte dei Marmi in Tuscany. There's a definite rock edge, with velvet ballerinas and brocade Moroccan pochettes thrown in for good measure.

Glamour in Rose, Via San Marco, 1, 02 6379 3540, Mon 3.30–7.30 pm, Tues–Sat 10 am – 7.30 pm. **www.glamourinrose.com**

L'Autre Chose (womenswear)

L'Autre Chose mixes the best of Made in Italy craftsmanship with creativity, elegance, a little bit of retro and a liberal dose of eccentricity through fabric, print, colour and retro-inspired shoes. It's Italian quality with a French touch, slightly Bohemian Parisienne with tailored suits and printed dresses and a decisive use of colour, and it's no surprise that it's a favourite with the fashion world. Check out their silk prints and T-bar shoes.

L'Autre Chose, Via Manzoni, 27, angolo Via Croce Rossa, Fiori Chiari, 16, 02 3670 8738, Mon – Sat 10.30 am – 7.30 pm, Sun 11 am – 7 pm. **www.lautrechose.com**

Luisa Beccaria (womenswear)

Luisa Beccaria designs the dreamiest dresses in exquisite fabrics, whether for everyday (although it's difficult to think

Luisa Beccaria. Luisa Beccaria

of Beccaria's dresses as for just everyday) or for that special occasion. The ethereal evening gowns and bridal dresses speak of romance and other worlds. Femininity is key, along with the use of high quality fabrics to create dresses that have been shown in art galleries and gardens. Luisa Beccaria was born in Milan and married a Sicilian nobleman, Lucio Bonaccorsi, and it's this constant dialogue between Milan and Sicily that she believes informs her work. She began to design dresses during the 1980s and in 1991 showed her first haute couture collection in Rome and Paris. Beccaria's daughter, Lucilla Bonaccorsi, joined her in 2006, while two of her other children Lucrezia and Ludovico have LùBar along Corso Venezia. (She has five children in total.) Her dresses are worn and loved by women such as Kate Winslet, Nicole Kidman, Sarah Jessica Parker and others. Come here, and be enchanted.

Madame Pauline Vintage. Rachael Martin

Luisa Beccaria, Via Marco Formentini, 1, 02 801417, Mon–Sat 10 am – 7 pm, Sun 11 am – 2 pm, 3–7 pm.
www.luisabeccaria.it

Madame Pauline (women's vintage clothing and accessories)

The feel is distinctly French, rather like a French boudoir, and hardly surprising for a shop that took its name in homage to Pauline Bonaparte, Napoleon's sister. The link is the elegant avenue where the shop is found: Foro Buonaparte is named after the man himself. Clothes, jewellery, hats and stoles all date from

Cecilia di Lorenzo

VINTAGE IN MILAN: CECILIA DI LORENZO

'I think, especially in Milan that's this cosmopolitan, open city, vintage has increased in importance in terms of the amount of vintage clothing and accessories that is being sold. Firstly, because there's this question of colour and image that's relevant to the fashion of today. You only have to think of Gucci, and it's all there, the long 1970s dresses, prints, floral pattern, stripes and so on. Today's fashion is full of colour with lurex, sequins, a strong return to the 1970s and the glamour of the 1940s. Vintage is also popular because women are paying more attention to environmental issues and as a result they're shopping more carefully and are aware of the aspect of recycling. While this was already felt in northern Europe twenty to thirty years ago, it's now being felt here in Lombardy. The cosmopolitan Milanese woman of today mixes vintage with maybe a new coat and creates a vintage look. And this is why vintage is so strong at the moment.'

the beginning of the twentieth century onwards, including costume jewellery by Elsa Schiaparelli and Coppola e Toppo. Their most recent items are all designer pieces and include Prada, Chanel, Hermès, Yves Saint Laurent and Marni alongside exquisite Valentino dresses, and 1970s long dresses with signature geometric prints, collars and cuffs. Upstairs they have an extensive archive with pieces that have been chosen with regards to stylistic value and include iconic couture and ready-to-wear pieces from fashion greats such as Valentino, Yves Saint Laurent and Ossie Clark. There are also pieces by Germana Marucelli, Gigliola Curiel, the Fontana Sisters, Antonelli, Walter Albini, Alberto Fabiani, Simonetta, Biki, Jole Veneziani, Emilio Schuberth, Emilio Pucci and Irene Galitzine. Lose yourself within 1920s and 1930s dresses, an incredible 1980s black Krizia jumpsuit, and a selection of all the biggest names in international couture. Archive pieces are available for rent upon request.

Madame Pauline, Foro Buonaparte, 74, 02 4943 1201, Mon 12.30–2 pm, 3–7.30 pm, Tues–Sun 10 am – 2pm, 3–7.30 pm. **www. madamepaulinevintage.it**

Slam Jam (men's streetwear)

Slam Jam is the company from Ferrara that was founded in 1989 before the term 'streetwear' even existed. It was underground, brought together fashion, art, music and clubbing, and was the first Italian importer of Stüssy, the

Californian surf brand that spread to streetwear and the hip hop scene. The emphasis at the store is on the best in US and Japanese streetwear, relevant art and music, and they often hold events.

Slam Jam, Via Giovanni Lanza, 1, 02 8909 3965, Mon 3.30–7.30 pm, Tues–Sat 11.30 am – 7.30 pm, Sun 3.30–7.30 pm. **www.slamjam.com**

Vintage Delirium by Franco Jacassi (women's and men's vintage clothing)

Vintage Delirium is the historic vintage shop and archive that's been here since 1985. It's famous for its enormous collection of buttons, possibly the largest in the world and certainly one of the most renowned. Then there are fabrics, embroidery, drawings, and of course the clothes and accessories. Some designers go to research fabrics, others go because they're interested in seeing how clothes were made. Clothes and accessories date from the end of the nineteenth century through to 1920s/1930s models by Chanel, Vionnet, Schiaparelli and Callot Soeurs. Look out for 1950s and 1960s clothing by Pucci, Dior, Cardin and Balenciaga, while the 1970s and 1980s includes pieces by Yves Saint Laurent, Versace and Mila Schön. The collection leads right up to the 1990s, with a special interest in 1990s Versace, Thierry Mugler and Azzedine Alaïa. 1990s fashion, that golden age when supermodels were striding down the catwalks wearing some of the best of Italian fashion, has never lost

its touch. For accessories, there's a selection including scarves, ribbons, ties, handbags and more that could keep you browsing for hours.

Vintage Delirium by Franco Jacassi, Via Giuseppe Sacchi, 3, 02 8646 2076, Mon–Fri 10 am – 7 pm, Sat 10.30 am–7 pm. **www.vintagedelirium.it**

ALSO VISIT...

Olfattorio bar à parfum is fun if you want to make up your own individually tailored perfume. For jewellery, go to **Angela Caputi Giuggiù** and check out the creations in resin that fuse colour and shape in the most beautiful of ways. **Manee** sells shoes for men, women and children including sneakers and fun eccentric brogues, while **Massimo Alba** specialises in cashmere and unstructured tailoring for both men and women.

Angela Caputi Giuggiù, Via Madonnina, 11, 02 8646 1080, Tues–Sat 10 am – 1 pm, 2.30 – 7.30 pm. **www.angelacaputi.com**

Manee, Via Madonnina, 10, 02 3659 0226, Mon 3 – 7 pm, Tues–Sat 10.30 am – 2 pm, 3 – 7 pm. **www.maneemilano.it**

Massimo Alba, Via Brera, 8, 02 7209 3420, Mon–Sat 10 am – 7 pm, Sun 2– 7 pm. **www.massimoalba.com**

Olfattorio, Via Brera, 5, 02 3653 2901, Mon–Sun 10.30 am – 7.30 pm. **www.olfattorio.it**

Rachael Martin

VIA SOLFERINO AND VIA DELLA MOSCOVA

For many years Via Solferino was mainly associated with being the home of Italian national newspaper *Il Corriere della Sera*. It still is, but it now has a lot to offer in terms of fashion, and also food. Its bars and restaurants are popular places in the evenings, the kind of place where you'll just want to hang around and watch the beautiful people at play. This is the place where that girl standing outside the café who looks like she's dressed in head-to-toe Gucci very probably is. It's also one of Milan's most desirable areas to live. Just don't expect anything particularly edgy; this all comes with a certain patina of the genteel.

EAT AND DRINK

LUNCH

Fioraio Bianchi Caffè

Peeling plaster walls, antique furniture and flowers, flowers everywhere, in homage to its original role as a florist's. Fioraio Bianchi Caffè brings a touch of Paris, with its Parisian-style bistrot and a menu that's classically Italian.

Fioraio Bianchi Caffè, Via Montebello, 7, 02 02 2901 4390, Mon–Sat 8 am – 12 am. **www. fioraiobianchicaffe.it**

Dry Milano Cocktails and Pizza

Twin a cocktail aperitivo with that old classic, pizza.

Dry Milano Cocktails and Pizza, Via Solferino, 33, 02 6379 3414, pizzeria: Tues–Sun 7 pm – 12 am, cocktail bar: 7 pm – 2 am.
www.drymilano.it

I Salentini

A piece of Puglia's Salento region in Milan with orecchiette, burrata and plenty of fish.

I Salentini, Via Solferino, 44, 02 4549 8948, Mon–Sun 11.30 pm – 3 pm, 6.30–11.30 pm (closed Monday lunchtime).
www.isalentini.com

SHOPPING

Giolina e Angelo (jewellery)

Handcrafted jewellery from the family business run by Angelo Mereu, who has more than forty years' experience of working in the jewellery sector. Giolina e Angelo opened in 2004. Mereu is known as the man who invented the nylon-thread bracelet, which forms the basis for many of the pieces here. He now works with daughter Giolina and son Giammarco and together they create refined and essential pieces that are loved by the Milanese, Italian celebrities and many more. Their range of jewellery includes delicate contemporary style gold, white gold, gilded

Giolina e Angelo

Giolina e Angelo

and silver pieces, including bracelets and necklaces with various charms.

Giolina e Angelo, Via Solferino, 22/A, 02 653770 Tues–Sat 10.30 am – 1.30 pm, 3–7 pm.
www.giolinaeangelo.com

Goods (womenswear)

Goods have basic items, unique pieces and collections all by Italian and international designers, including cashmere jumpers and vintage handbags. They also sell their own collection of blouses, skirts and dresses in Como silk and have a tailor-made service where the customer chooses colour and model according to personal taste. The shop is just a short walk from Via Solferino in premises by interior designer Pietro Castagna.

Goods, Via Castelfidardo, 02 3659 6003, Mon 2–8 pm, Tues–Sat 10.30 am – 8 pm.
www.goodsmilano.it

L'Artigiano di Brera (shoes)

L'Artigiano di Brera is a family business that has been selling artisan-made shoes for roughly half a century. Their sizes range from 30 to 43 and they have ballerinas in virtually every colour you can imagine, including Roger Vivier inspired Pilgrim pumps in various colours and materials.

L'Artigiano di Brera, Via Solferino, 1, 02 8058 1910, Mon 3.30 – 7.30 pm, Tues–Sat 10.30 am – 2 pm, 3–7.30 pm.
www.lartigianodibrera.com

La Tenda (womenswear)

Marco Longoni opened his first La Tenda boutique in 1965 in Via Plinio, 13. The Via Solferino boutique was his second. It's been a reference point of Milanese fashion for years, and is now run by sons Vittorio and Stefano. The concept behind the store is to offer not only a boutique, but a shopping experience that fuses art, fashion and culture. Brands stocked

include Avant Toi, Giorgio Brato and Isabel Benenato.

La Tenda, Via Solferino, 10, Mon–Sat 10 am – 7 pm, Sun 11 am – 2 pm, 3 – 7 pm.
www.latendamilano.com

Le Solferine (shoes and accessories)

Le Solferine is all about the shoes, or rather Silvia Bertolaja's creations that bring back the pleasure of dressing up. In fact, this is Silvia's philosophy: the art of dressing up. Go for heels, thigh-high boots or glamourous sandals. They also have Le Vintage in Isola where they sell retro-inspired clothing. (see page 149)

Le Solferine, Via Solferino, 2, 02 655 5352, Mon 11am – 7.30 pm, Tues–Sat 10 am – 7.30 pm, Sun 11 am – 2 pm, 3 – 7 pm. **www.lesolferine.com**

Ottico Marchesi (eyewear)

Eyewear store Ottico Marchesi has been in Brera since 1959. Just don't expect the usual designer frames. Of course some of them are here, but once you see the handmade ones made in Veneto, chances are you too will fall in love.

Ottico Marchesi, Via Solferino, 11, 02 86461378, Mon 3–7pm, Tues–Fri 10 am – 7pm, Sat 10 am – 1 pm, 3.30 pm – 7 pm.
www.otticamarchesi.com

ALSO VISIT…
Blue Deep is a go-to for many, and sells a curated selection of Made in Italy clothing and accessories brands.

Also go to **Kristina Ti**, very popular with the Milanese, for Boho-chic Italian style, while **L'Arabesque** is the smaller boutique of the store in Largo Augusto. Go for retro-style women's clothing and accessories and design items that fuse eastern spirit with western lines. Italian womenswear line **Maliparmi** is another favourite for Milanese chic with an emphasis on colour, print and embroidery. Venetian menswear company **Slowear** offer precisely that: slow wear, durable fashion with a focus on quality and craftsmanship. Go for Glanshirt shirts, Zanone jumpers and Incotex chinos.

Blue Deep, Via Solferino, 5 02 876702, Mon 11 am – 7.30 pm, Tues – Sat 10.30 am – 7.30 pm. **www.bluedeepstore.com**

Kristina T, Via Solferino, 18, 02 653379, Mon 3 – 7 pm, Tues–Sat 10 am – 7 pm. **www.kristinati.it**

L'Arabesque, Largo Treves, 1, 02 8646 2847, Mon–Sat 10.30 am – 7 pm. **www.larabesque.net**

Maliparmi, Via Solferino, 3, 02 7209 3899 Mon–Sun 10 am – 7 pm. **www.maliparmi.com**

Slowear, Via Solferino, 18, 02 6347 1384, Mon–Sat 10.30 am – 7.30 pm, Sun 11 am – 8 pm. **www.slowear.com**.

FOCUS ON BOUTIQUE FASHION

When Giovanni Battisti Giorgini showed Italian fashion to an audience of American buyers and journalists at the first Italian High Fashion show in Florence in 1951, he also introduced the concept of high quality ready-to-wear Italian boutique fashion such as that made by Emilio Pucci. Boutique fashion was different, and more importantly, it was something that the French weren't doing. This concept of the boutique, the idea of going into a trusted shop filled with carefully selected items upon which you will be carefully advised and come out with a finished complete look, remains strong.

Women take their daughters as if it were a rite of passage. Offer just the right service, and you'll keep your clients for years. Legendary Milanese boutiques include Biffi Boutique (see page 160), Gio Moretti (see page 59), Imarika (see page 130), and Pupi Solari (see page 143) for children. Then there's Atelier Bergnach (see page 129) where Elena Bergnach makes her own skirts and provides other items to complete the look.

Do check out Wait and See (see page 117) in Milan's historical city centre for a fashion take on their philosophy, 'la vita è bella'.

If you're down around Porta Romana, call in at MaClò. Brazilian born Patricia Pauliv's boutique mixes Italian and French clothing brands with an overall French feel that comes from the touches of embroidery on garments and bags, softly cut shapes, roomy jumpers, polka-dots and horizontal stripes. Pieces may be classic but always have an individual touch, whether it be detailing on a blouse or the cut of a pair of trousers. Her emphasis is always upon offering a boutique service, ensuring that each customer is advised, without being pressured, and that they leave her shop feeling 'ready'. And it evidently works, as customers come back again and again.

DUOMO
Shopping and culture in Milan's historical centre

M1 / M3 Duomo, M1 San Babila

The Piazza del Duomo is home to Milan's Duomo (cathedral) and has some of the city's most important sights. The main fashion attraction here is the stunning nineteenth-century Galleria Vittorio Emanuele II, one of Europe's oldest malls, which inspired other similar malls such as the Galleria Umberto I in Naples. It links Piazza del Duomo with Piazza della Scala, home to Milan's world-famous opera house La Scala, Gallerie d'Italia, with its collection of nineteenth- and twentieth-century Italian and Lombard painting, and the city hall Palazzo Marino. Corso Vittorio Emanuele II is the elegant street full of high street names that leads off Piazza del Duomo and along to Piazza San Babila. Via Torino goes from the Piazza del Duomo towards Corso di Porta Ticinese and has plenty of high street names. The pedestrianised Via Dante, with its cafés and tables outside, leads

Galleria Vittorio Emanuele II.

to the Castello Sforzesco, Milan's Sforza Castle.

Nearby Piazza Mercanti was the centre of medieval Milan, where merchants used to meet and justice was done. The streets leading off this square were famous for quality craftsmanship right up to the 1600s. If you were a European prince or knight, this was the place to come and get your armour. Via Orefici was where the goldsmiths worked and Via Armorari was home to the armourers. Via Speronari takes its name from the workshops that made equipment for horses and helmets. Via dei Spadari, where they used to make swords, now has Peck, one of Milan's ultimate food shopping experiences. A heaven for foodies, it's the trusted delicatessen of the Milanese with a gastronomic café that does great breakfasts and aperitifs.

Peck, Via Spadari, 9, 02 802 3161, Mon 3-8 pm, Tues–Sat 9 am – 8 pm, Sun 10 am – 5 pm. **www.peck.it** (Check website for summer opening hours as they may be closed on Sundays.)

EAT AND DRINK

COFFEE

Pasticceria Marchesi

Go for breakfast at Marchesi 1824, situated high above the Galleria, with views looking down over the Galleria, exquisite retro furnishings, pastel-coloured cakes and other goodies in beautiful little boxes that you'll want to take home. Stand at the bar and have your cappuccino and brioche, or sit down in plush green velvet chairs and watch it all unfold before you. They even have a cooked breakfast option, should you fancy it. Ask for the menu in English.

Pasticceria Marchesi, Galleria Vittorio Emaneuele II, 02 9418 1710, Mon–Sun 7.30 am – 9 pm. **www.pasticceriamarchesi.com**

LUNCH

Café Trussardi

The subtle clean lines of Café Trussardi form the perfect backdrop for Patrick Blanc's 'soffitto vegetale' that hangs from the roof.

Café Trussardi, Piazza della Scala, 5, 02 8068 8295, Mon–Fri 7.30 am – 11 pm, Sat 12 pm – 11 pm. **www.trussardi.com**

Miss Sixty Café

Go for breakfast, lunch or cocktails at the pop-art inspired Miss Sixty Café within the Miss Sixty flagship store. The theme is pink, with pink velvet sofas, tables and cappuccinos. When it opened in 2019, the wallpaper of exotic plants with a pink background was one of Milan's top Instagram images.

Miss Sixty Café, Piazza del Duomo, 31, 02 8632 23379, Mon–Sun 11 am – 9 pm. **www.misssixty.com**

Signorvino

Signorvino, or 'Mr Wine' in English, is a wine bar with food that overlooks the

Duomo. Go for bruschetta, cheese and cold meat platters, pasta, soups and tapas-style aperitivo. They also organise wine tastings, and have an extensive selection of wine available to buy. Check their website for details.

Signorvino, Piazza del Duomo, corner Corso Vittorio Emanuele II, 02 8909 2539, Mon–Sun 12 pm – 11 pm (enoteca opens at 9 am). **www.signorvino.com**

APERITIVO

Cracco

Head to Cracco for a spritz in the Galleria Vittorio Emanuele II. Carlo Cracco is the Italian celebrity chef whose restaurant offers gourmet Italian cuisine.

Cracco, Galleria Vittorio Emanuele II, 02 876774, café Mon–Sun 8 am – 12 am, restaurant Mon–Fri 12.30–2 pm, 7.15–10 pm, Sat 7.30–10 pm. For the restaurant, you'll need to book. **www.ristorantecracco.it**

Terazza Aperol

High up in the Galleria, with views facing right out onto Piazza Duomo, this is a classic destination on any tourist itinerary.

Terazza Aperol, Piazza del Duomo corner Galleria Vittorio Emanuele, 335 7356773, Sun–Fri 11 am – 11 pm, Sat 11 am – 1 am. **www.aperol.com**

CULTURE STOP

Castello Sforzesco

Milan's fifteenth-century Sforza Castle, originally a Visconti family fortress, was home to the Sforza family, Milan's ruling dynasty from 1450 until 1535. Beatrice d'Este, daughter of Ercole I d'Este, Duke of Ferrara, lived here after she married

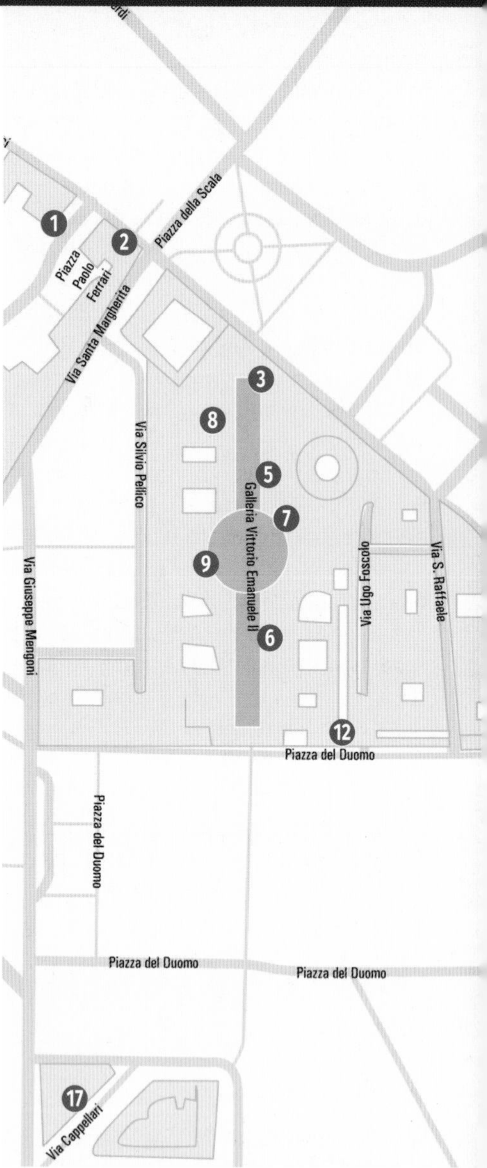

THE CENTRE. 1 Porselli, 2 Trussardi, 3 Borsalino, 4 Chanel, 5 Gucci, 6 Libreria Bocca, 7 Louis Vuitton, 8 Piumelli, 9 Versace, 10 Max & Co, 11 Max Mara, 12 Tiffany & Co, 13 United Colours of Benetton, 14 L'Arabesque, 15 Rinascente, 16 Humana Vintage, 17 Foto Veneta Ottica.

CRAFTSMANSHIP AND QUALITY TEXTILES ARE ROOTED IN THE RENAISSANCE

Textiles played a huge role in the economies of cities like Florence, Rome, Milan, and the ports of Genoa and Venice, and costumes in Renaissance paintings show exquisite velvets, linens, wools, and if you were really lucky, silks. Fashion was a serious (and highly competitive) business during Renaissance times. Clothing had always been a display of status, wealth and political power, and during the Renaissance it became a question of taste. Italy was already gaining a reputation for the high quality of its textiles. Florence and Milan were the main production centres, and both the Florentine and Milanese courts set the standards throughout Europe. Sisters Beatrice d'Este and Isabella d'Este were both Renaissance fashion influencers amid Europe's noblewomen and royalty, although it was reputed that Beatrice had the advantage in terms of quantity of dresses and sheer splendour. Beatrice had married Ludovico Sforza and became Duchess of Milan, while Isabella d'Este had married into the Gonzaga family and became Marchioness of Mantua. Later, during the eighteenth century, Louis XIV came along and stole the fashion limelight, and right up until after the Second World War, Paris dictated fashion. The Italians would buy their models from France and copy French designs at a time before originality became an essential quality. 'Modellista' was the person, often a woman, whose job it was to copy the designs. Yet it was always the craftsmanship that marked the garments out, along with the quality of materials.

Ludovico Sforza in 1491 when she was only 15. She became a fashion icon of the Sforza court for the short time she lived here before her death in childbirth at the age of 21.

Castello Sforzesco, Piazza Castello, 02 8846 3703, Mon–Sun 7 am – 7.30 pm; museum, Tues–Sun 9 am – 5.30pm. **www.milanocastello.it**

Duomo

Building was begun in 1386 upon the orders of Gian Galeazzo Visconti, first Duke of Milan, and lasted 500 years. The pink marble used from Candoglia was brought along the Navigli, the city's canal system. At the very top of the cathedral is the statue of the Madonnina, inextricably linked to Milanese culture and affectionately sung about in Giovanni D'Anzi's 1935 song 'O

Piazza del Duomo.

Adobe Stock

Roof terraces of Milan's Duomo.

mia bèla Madunina', Milanese dialect for 'my beautiful Madonnina'. Go up to the terraces for stunning views of the Torre Velasca, the Porta Nuova skyline and the Alps on a clear day. You'll get the best views in winter, although if it's icy, the terraces may be closed.

Duomo di Milano, Piazza del Duomo, see **www.duomomilano.it** for entry times as these can vary.

Gallerie d'Italia

Home to the nineteenth- and twentieth-century Italian art collections of Intesa San Paolo and Fondazione Cariplo banks.

Gallerie d'Italia, Piazza della Scala, 6, Tues–Sun 9.30 am – 7.30 pm (Thursdays open till 10.30 pm). **www.gallerieditalia.com**

Museo del Novecento

Brush up on twentieth-century Italian art at the Novecento museum. Head up

to the Lucio Fontana room for Fontana's *Structure in Neon* against fantastic views of the Pizza del Duomo.

Museo del Novecento, Via Giuglielmo Marconi, 1, 02 8844 4061, Mon 2.30–7.30 pm, Tues/Wed/Fri/Sun 9.30 am – 7.30 pm, Thurs/Sat 9.30 am – 10.30 pm. **www.museodelnovecento.org**

Palazzo Reale

Seat of the city's government under the fourteenth- and fifteenth-century Visconti and Sforza families, today the palace hosts many exhibitions, including ones that are related to fashion and fashion photography. Check in advance to see what's on.

Palazzo Reale, Piazza Duomo, 12, Mon 2.30–7.30 pm, Tues–Fri 9.30 am – 7.30 pm, Sat 9.30 am – 10.30 pm.
www.palazzorealemilano.it

Osservatorio Fondazione Prada

The Osservatorio Fondazione Prada is the Fondazione Prada's exhibition space dedicated to contemporary photography and visual languages. The 880-square-metre gallery is high up in the Galleria Vittorio Emanuele II above the Prada Uomo boutique, in a space that was bombed in 1943 but has now been completely restored. Its ground floor entrance is the same as that for Pasticceria Marchesi, only in this case you'll need to take the lift.

Osservatorio Fondazione Prada, Galleria Vittorio Emanuele II, Mon/Wed/Thurs/Fri 2–8pm, Sat–Sun 11 am – 8 pm.
www.fondazioneprada.org

Teatro alla Scala

Book in advance if you want to see a performance at the world famous La Scala opera house, designed by Giuseppe Piermarini. The museum has a permanent collection and hosts temporary exhibitions.

Teatro alla Scala, Piazza Scala.
www.teatroallascala.org

Museo Teatrale alla Scala, Piazza Scala, Mon–Sun 9 am – 5.30 pm. **www.museoscala.org**

TEATRO ALLA SCALA AND THE MILANESE COUTURIERS

On 7 December 1951 Maria Callas appeared in the opening night of Verdi's *'Sicilian Vespers'* at Teatro alla Scala. Her performance was a success, and that evening she met Biki at the house of the famous composer Wally Toscanini. Biki, as Elvira Leonardi Bouyeure was known, was familiar with the world of the opera house because she'd grown up in it. (Her grandmother was the wife of composer Giacomo Puccini.) The first time Callas presented herself in Biki's studio, Biki wasn't impressed and told her to come back when she'd lost weight. So Callas did, and then went back. Biki not only dressed Callas, but taught her how to dress, down to little handwritten notes that she gave Callas to put in her suitcase when she travelled, which told her what to wear with what. Biki helped to transform Callas into the diva known as *'la divina'* (the divine), and earn her place in the American press's

Teatro alla Scala.

list of the ten best-dressed women in the world. 'La Callas', as she was known, was an opera diva like no one else, and through her, Biki helped Milan establish a reputation for fashion.

The opening night at Teatro alla Scala of 7 December, the same day as the Milan's patron saint, Sant'Ambrogio, brought a cultural rebirth of opera and fashion in a Milan that still had fresh memories of the Second World War. Post-war reconstruction of Italy led to economic boom, particularly in Milan. Teatro alla Scala was the setting that bridged the old with the new, mixed a world of aristocrats and upper-class families with new money, film stars and politicians. While the rest of the year the Milanese society ladies may have kept

it all understated with a certain sense of restraint, the opening night of Teatro alla Scala was the night they dressed up, and it mattered.

This relationship between La Scala and fashion lasted all through the 1950s and 1960s. Designers such as Gigliola Curiel, Jole Veneziana, Germana Marucelli and Mila Schön were all responsible for dressing the Milanese ladies, while others designed for the productions themselves. 1968 brought social change, and protests were directed at La Scala as a symbol of the Milanese elite. Yet La Scala has retained its place as an emblem of Milanese culture throughout the world. The link between fashion and opera is strong. Versace designed for Maurice Béjart, the French-born opera director. Armani, Ottavio Missoni and Karl Lagerfeld also designed costumes for the theatre. Dolce & Gabbana held their fall/winter 2016 Alta Moda collection at La Scala, inspired by the world of opera and Biki. It was a collection fit for any diva to theatrically die for: bejewelled, highly embroidered fur trims, elaborate headpieces and the most exquisite cocktail dresses. The grand finale was to the sounds of Puccini's *'Nessun Dorma'*. Guests were dressed in Dolce & Gabbana haute couture. This was glorious, emotional, Italian couture, which tapped into the Italian canons of opera, culture and history. Needless to say, the audience of fashion editors and couture clients loved it.

PIAZZA DELLA SCALA

M1 Duomo, M3 Montenapoleone

SHOPPING

Porselli (classical dance shoes and accessories, ballerina shoes)

Opened in 1919 by Eugenio Porselli, Porselli have been supplying pointe shoes to La Scala ballet students ever since, and exporting them all over the world. They have everything for the dance world, including jazz and flamenco shoes. They also have a selection of variations on the ballerina flat in a wide range of colours.

Porselli, Piazza Paolo Ferrari, 6, 02 805 3759 Mon 3 – 7.30 pm, Tues – Sat 9 am – 12.30 pm, 3 – 7.30 pm. **www.porselli.it**

Trussardi (womenswear, menswear, childrenswear)

Dante Trussardi began making luxury leather gloves in Bergamo in 1911, achieved international success and became official supplier to the British royal family. The first boutique opened in Milan in 1976 along Via Sant'Andrea, and the company became one of the key Italian fashion brands of the 1980s, also through its collaborations with brands such as Alitalia, Alfa Romeo, Agusta and Garelli. It was the first fashion house to open fashion shows to the public when it decided to show its fall/winter collection in Piazza del Duomo in 1984. The premises here opened in 1996, with boutique, showroom, Café Trussardi and the restaurant Trussardi alla Scala. Trussardi remains a prestigious luxury lifestyle brand that's well-known for its elegant, understated style and quality.

Trussardi, Piazza della Scala, 5, 02 8068 8242, Mon–Sun 10 am – 8 pm. **www.trussardi.com**;

Café Trussardi, Piazza della Scala, 5, 02 8068 8295, Mon–Fri 7.30 am – 11 pm, Sat noon – 11 pm; **Il Ristorante Trussardi alla Scala,** Piazza della Scala, 5, 02 8068 8201, lunch Mon–Fri 12.30 – 2.30 pm, dinner Mon–Sat 8–10.30 pm. **www.trussardiallascala.com**

GALLERIA VITTORIO EMANUELE II

It's 1867. The Galleria Vittorio Emanuele II has just been inaugurated, in spite of recent tragedy. (Giuseppe Mengoni, to whose design it was built, fell from the scaffolding and died just days before.) The Kingdom of Italy was proclaimed just six years ago, and the current king, Vittorio Emanuele II, will reign for another eleven years. Europe is upon the eve of the Belle Époque, with its focus on Paris. It's a time that will herald a period of arts, architecture such as Art Nouveau, known in Italy as Stile Liberty (Liberty style), and inventions that will change the face of modern society, while Puccini will write 'La Bohème' and put the bohemian way of life on stage. The Galleria quickly becomes a meeting place for the Milanese bourgeoisie. In 1878 Umberto I inherits the throne as Umberto I of Italy, rather than Umberto IV of Savoy. His wife is Queen Margherita, fashion icon and intellectual, famed for her love of pearls and precious jewels. People begin to speak of what is known as the 'Margherita style', which encompasses clothing, entertaining and food. Her husband undertakes numerous affairs and it's rumoured that the beauty of her jewels is related to

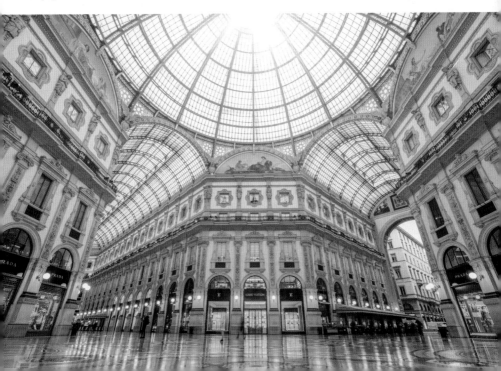

how much he needs to be forgiven.

The restoration of the Galleria by Prada and Versace was completed in April 2015 in time for Expo 2015. The work began in March 2014 and the year-long restoration revealed original two-colour façades. This isn't the only time that the fashion world has given funds for Italy's historic monuments. Giorgio Armani sponsored the restoration of Villa Necchi Campiglio, Fendi gave money to restore five fountains in Rome, including the Trevi Fountain, and Tod's to resoration work on the Colosseum.

The atmosphere in the Galleria today is still very special, and recalls memories of a more recent past. Verdi, Toscanini and Carrà drank at the Camparino bar. Maria Callas, Charlie Chaplin, Frank Sinatra, Ava Gardner, Prince Rainier and Princess Grace of Monaco dined at the historic Savini, while Hemingway and Toscanini drank

LUISA CASATI

Born in Milan in 1881, Luisa Casati, or the Marchesa Casati Stampa di Soncino as she became through marriage, was the heiress and muse who broke all the rules. She was the daughter of Albert Amman and Lucia Bressi. Amman was of Austrian origin, Bressi was born in Vienna, and Casati grew up within a culturally lively household during the time of the Milanese fin de siècle. When Casati was only a teenager she and her sister were orphaned, became two of the richest women in Italy, and thus infinitely desirable. Casati married Marquess Camillo Casati Stampa di Soncino in 1900. Shortly after, in 1903, she met Italian poet Gabriele D'Annunzio and their affair dramatically changed her, beginning her transformation from newly married wealthy daughter of Milanese industrialists, to extravagant fashion icon. Needless to say, respectable married life didn't suit her. Casati moved to Venice to live at the Palazzo Venier dei Leoni on the Grand Canal, that later became home of the Peggy Guggenheim collection.

Casati loved fashion, including Fortuny and Poiret. Legend has it that she used the juice of belladonna or deadly nightshade to make her eyes darker and her pupils more dilated. Women have always gone to great lengths for fashion, and the practice was not uncommon in Italy at the time. Stories abound of Casati walking through Venice, wearing only fur coat and heavy make up, and leading her leopards on jewel-encrusted leads. At other times she wore her boa constrictor as a necklace. Casati said she wanted to be a living work of art, and attracted attention wherever she went, despite apparently being incredibly shy. During the 1930s the press claimed she was 'the most daring and extravagant woman in the world'. Many painted and photographed her, including Man Ray, Giacomo Balla and Cecil Beaton. She was adored by the Italian Futurists, and was muse to Karl Lagerfeld, John Galliano, Alexander McQueen, Tom Ford and Dries van Noten. She also inspired the name of Georgina Chapman and Keren Craig's fashion house, Marchesa.

at Biffi. This stunning iron structure with its glass roof still contains the shops with their characteristic signs of distinctive gold writing on a black background. Some of the historic shops are still here. Famous milliner Borsalino began near Alessandria in 1857 making the hats that are now iconic, and also available in bright funky colours that are perfect for brightening up any grey day. Libreria Bocca was started in 1775 in Turin by the Bocca brothers and is one of Europe's oldest bookshops. Piumelli started out in 1958 making beautifully finished leather gloves for both men and women. They then branched out into bags and small leather goods. Many others have left and the fashion houses have moved in including Louis Vuitton, Gucci, Versace and the first Chanel beauty store in Milan.

Do go to Prada. Miuccia Prada's grandfather, Mario, opened his luggage and luxury goods company here in 1913 and in 1919 Prada became official supplier to the Italian royal family. It was during this time that one of Prada's bestselling (and oldest) bags, the 'Saffiano', or 'Galleria bag' as it is sometimes also known, was designed and patented. Made with the highest quality calf leather, it takes its name from its cross hatch print. The shop still retains original fittings, including the original mahogany shelves that were designed and produced by a British architect while the cabinet downstairs

Adobe Stock

Seal of Turin mosaic in the Galleria Vittorio Emanuele II.

contains early twentieth-century items.

Don't forget the Galleria's central Seal of Turin mosaic. If you spin round three times in an anti-clockwise direction on the bull's testicles, it's said to bring good luck. To walk the galleria's highline, high up on its roofs, see **www. highlinegalleria.com**.

Borsalino, Galleria Vittorio Emanuele II, 92, 02 8901 5436, Mon–Sat 10 am – 7 pm Sun 10 am – 2 pm, 3 – 7 pm. **www.borsalino.com**

Chanel, Corso Vittorio Emanuele II, 14, 02 2908 9581, Mon–Sat 10 am – 7 pm, Sun 11am – 7.30 pm. **www.chanel.com**

Gucci, Corso Vittorio Emanuele II, 02 859 7991, Mon–Sat 10 am – 7.30 pm, Sun 10 am – 7 pm. **www.gucci.com**

Libreria Bocca, Galleria Vittorio Emanuele II, 02 8646 2321, Mon – Sun 10am – 7pm. **www.libreriabocca.com**

Louis Vuitton, Galleria Vittorio Emanuele II, 02 7214 7011, Mon–Sat 10 am – 7.30 pm, Sun 10.30 am – 7.30 pm. **www.louisvuitton.com**

Piumelli, Galleria Vittorio Emanuele II, 02 869 2318, Mon–Sun 10 am – 7.30 pm. **www.piumelli.com**

Prada, Galleria Vittorio Emanuele II, 02 876979, Mon-Sat 10 am – 7.30 pm, Sun 10am – 7pm. **www.prada.com**

Versace, Galleria Vittorio Emanuele II, 33/35, 02 8901 1469, Mon–Sat 10 am – 7.30 pm, Sun 10 am – 7 pm. **www.versace.com**

CORSO VITTORIO EMANUELE II

M1 Duomo, M1 San Babila

In 1845 Charles Dickens, in his travelogue *Pictures from Italy,* described the carriages carrying nobles along this prestigious avenue leading out from Piazza del Duomo, commenting that rather than give up their public promenade, the nobles would rather half starve themselves, such was the importance of the public promenade. This promenade or afternoon

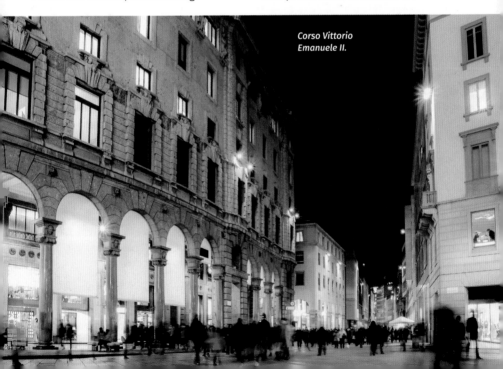

Corso Vittorio Emanuele II.

*Basilica di San Babila,
Piazza San Babila.*

passeggiata still continues, mainly on a Saturday afternoon, albeit in twenty-first-century form and with a contingency of tourists sitting at the tables of the restaurants and bars that line it. Up until the 1990s there were several cinemas along here. In the early half of the twentieth century, Piazza Cesare Beccaria, where the Galleria del Corso is now, was a famous meeting place for actors and artists, and home to various record companies. Nowadays you can take your pick of lots of familiar high street names, both higher-end brands and low-cost fashion. There are Italian high street staples such as the **Benetton** flagship store. The history of Benetton involves a family from Veneto, revolutionary fashion advertising and Formula 1 racing. Founded in 1965, its fortune came from the jumpers they produced that were dyed after the jumpers were made, and thus each individual model was presented in a range of colours. **MaxMara** and their younger line **Max & Co** are here too. Achille Maramotti started making couture in 1947, founded MaxMara in 1951 and was a keen advocate of mass-produced quality clothing. Max & Co is its younger line that's given a twist for the high street. Head to the famous department store **Rinascente**, and explore the various shopping arcades. The **Tiffany** flagship store is also along here. It hit the news in 2017 when it opened because of its prime location overlooking Piazza del Duomo and its status as the largest store in Europe.

Max & Co, Corso Vittorio Emanuele II, corner Piazza Liberty, 4, 02 780 433, Mon–Sun 10 am – 8 pm. **www.maxandco.com**

MaxMara, Piazza del Liberty / Corso Vittorio Emanuele II, 4, 02 7600 8849, Mon–Sun 10 am – 8 pm. **www.maxmara.com**

Tiffany & Co, Piazza del Duomo, corner Via Ugo Foscolo, 1, 02 8909 4202, Mon–Sun 10 am – 7.30 pm. **www.tiffany.com**

United Colours of Benetton, Corso Vittorio Emanuele II, 9, 02 7712 94209, Mon–Sun 10 am – 9 pm. **www.benetton.com**

L'Arabesque (concept store)

Not far from from Corso Vittorio Emanuele II and the Duomo, L'Arabesque is the cult concept store opened by stylist, designer and jewellery collector Chichi Meroni in 2010. The store places men's and women's fashion designed by owner Chichi Meroni alongside vintage pieces and vintage bijoux. There's also mid-century furniture that includes work by the most important Italian and foreign designers from the 1950s and 1960s, and Chichi Meroni's own design range 'The Wind Melody'. There is also

a bookshop with sourced books about fashion, photography, art, cinema and interiors and particularly those that you might not find elsewhere, alongside a restaurant serving traditional Italian cuisine, and a café.

L'Arabesque, Largo Augusto, 10, 02 7601 4825, Mon–Sat 10.30 am – 7 pm. **www.larabesque. net**

Rinascente

Much loved by the Milanese and tourists, Rinascente is Milan's oldest department store and still packs the charm after so many years. It was opened by the Bocconi brothers in 1865, under the name of Magazzini Bocconi. (The first European department store was Le Bon Marché that opened in Paris in 1838.) Stores in Rome, Trieste and Genoa followed, and in 1877 they opened Grandiosi Magazzini Aux Villes d'Italie. It became La Rinascente, the name given to it by the poet Gabriele D'Annunzio, when it was taken over in 1917. 'Rinascente' means resurgence or rebirth, and it was especially appropriate as several days after it opened in 1918 it was consumed by fire. When it opened again in 1921, in this sense it was indeed a resurgence.

Nowadays, the beautifully laid out areas hold all the big designer names, and it's a very popular tourist destination. You could easily spend a morning here followed by coffee or lunch. Eight floors sell all types of quality goods including fashion, homeware, accessories and cosmetics, and the seventh-floor food market stocks some of the best in Italian and international food. Also check out the Annex. It has collections by brands with a young appeal such as Urban Outfitters, who first opened here in Milan, Carhartt and others. Head for lunch at the top floor Maio Restaurant for Italian cooking with a modern twist. Their terrace is directly opposite the spires of the Duomo, and a very special place to enjoy lunch or dinner. They also have a wide selection of cocktails, perfect for an aperitivo.

Rinascente, Piazza del Duomo, 02 9138 7388, **www.rinascente.it**
The store is open seven days a week. Check their website for current opening hours as these can vary.

Maio Restaurant, Piazza del Duomo, (Rinascente Food Hall seventh floor), 02 8852 455, **www.maiorestaurant.com**
The whole of the Food Hall is open Mon-Sat 8.30 am – 12 am, Sunday 10am – 12 am.

PIAZZA SAN BABILA

M1 San Babila

1970s Piazza San Babila was where it was all happening, and its focus was a store named Fiorucci. Elio Fiorucci, a young Italian designer, went to London in 1965, discovered Biba and the boutique world of Swinging London and brought it back to Milan. In 1967 he opened his first store, Fiorucci, in the Galleria Passarella in Piazza San Babila, where he sold clothes by London designers such as Ossie Clark and Zandra Rhodes. The shop became a reference point for a generation. A second Milan store followed, and then in 1975 he opened on the King's Road in London. The Manhattan store followed in 1976 and it became known as the daytime Studio 54 after famous New York nightclub Studio 54. People would stop in the streets to watch the assistants dancing in the windows, and even Jackie Kennedy was known to have shopped there in private.

In 1984 Fiorucci invited Keith Haring to decorate the whole of the San Babila store. Haring worked straight through for two days, the store was kept open for the public to witness art in action and the result was appropriately iconic. Elio Fiorucci became known as the king of stretch jeans when, after seeing how wet jeans cling to a woman's body in Ibiza, he designed high-waisted stretch jeans that could only be fastened if you were lying on a bed. He was also renowned for his Victorian angels, net miniskirts and the leopard prints that had originally been made famous by Elsa Schiaparelli.

Fiorucci in San Babila represented a cultural reference point for a generation and a time, and then in 2003 it closed. Yet Fiorucci, with its mix of Italian cool and New York disco days, is back. A store opened in London's Soho in September 2017 under new owners Janie and Stephen Schaffer at a party that *Vogue* deemed

FOCUS ON DESIGN

Milan is the international capital of design with origins that lie in the first part of the 1900s and a history of design greats that includes Gio Ponti, Achille Castiglioni, Ettore Sottsass and Gae Aulenti. Just like the fashion world, the design world was backed by the industry of Milan's hinterland, while Milan's Triennale, which originally began at Monza's Villa Reale in 1923 as the Biennale or Biennal Exhibition of Decorative Arts in Monza, gave it an international showcase. Milan's Salone Internazionale del Mobile (international furniture fair) started in 1961. It takes place every April and is the largest and most important furniture fair in the world, showcasing the best in Italian design. It's at Fiera Milano Rho, where the whole city comes alive under the Fuorisalone programme which encompasses the worlds of design, fashion, and also food.

Via Durini, off Piazza San Babila, is the street of design, and a hotspot destination during Design Week with its showrooms of design brands such as B&B Italia, and Cassina, which was given a new interior by art director Patricia Urquiola fifty years after its opening. Go to Galleria Rossana Orlandi, owned by Rossana Orlandi. It showcases a selection of contemporary, vintage and emerging designers (see page 121). It's a must-visit during Design Week when 55,000 visitors pass through. Also take time to check out some of Milan's artisan workshops such as Laboratorio Paravicini and MV% Ceramics for beautifully decorated ceramics. (See page 116 and page 162)

B&B, Via Durini, 14, 02 764 4411, Mon 3 – 7 pm, Tues–Sat 10 am – 7 pm. **www.bebitalia.com**

Cassina, Via Durini, 16, 02 7602 0745, Mon – Fri 10 am – 7pm, Sat 10 am – 6 pm.
www.cassina.com

suitably worthy of the disco era. The store even has its own Paninaro Bar, a reference to the youth subculture known as 'paninari' who hung out in panino bars during the 1980s, wore brands such as Moncler puffer jackets and Best Company sweatshirts, and listened to bands such as Duran Duran.

This cult of the 'paninaro' was born in Milan, specifically at a bar named Al Panino in Piazza Liberty, moved into Piazza San Babila and in particular the fast-food bar Burghy, and spread to other cities all over Italy. It was all part of the years known as 'Milano da bere', years of economic affluence and hedonism that sought to break away from the politically difficult years of the 1970s. In 2010 the Fiorucci Art Trust was set up under artistic director Milovan Farronato, who also curated the Italy Pavilion at the Venice Biennale in 2019.

Not far from here is the Società del Giardino where Walter Albini held his first fashion show in 1971 after which *Women's Wear Daily* hailed him as the new Yves Saint Laurent. Born in Busto Arsizio in Lombardy in 1941, despite his family's plans for him to study classics, Albini enrolled at the Institute of Art, Design and Fashion in Turin. He was inspired by French couturier Poiret, and by the age of 17 he was providing sketches of high fashion shows for magazines and newspapers. Albini loved prêt-à-porter, and his belief in giving fashion to women at a more affordable price and revolutionary approach to fashion make him one of the most significant figures of Italian ready to wear. He died at the age of 42 in 1983.

VIA TORINO

M1 Duomo

Via Torino is the street that leads away from the centre and goes into Corso di Porta Ticinese and the Navigli area. It has a young feel with trendy shops and lots of streetwear. If you're with teenagers, they'll probably love it.

Humana Vintage (women's and men's vintage clothing)

For vintage clothing, head to Humana Vintage that's a block away from Via Torino, just off Via Mazzini near Piazza del Duomo. The company sells second-hand clothes to help finance development projects in the poorest countries of the world. They specialise in 1960s and 1970s clothing and accessories, and also sell wedding dresses.

Humana Vintage, Via Cappellari, 3, 02 7208 0606, Mon–Sat 10.30 am – 7.30 pm, Sun 11.30 am – 7 pm. **www.humanavintage.it**

Foto Veneta Ottica (eyewear)

The first floor of an eighteenth-century palazzo along Via Torino holds the shop that Gabriele Bisello started in 1931 when he opened a photography studio. 'Ottica' was added when son Giorgio became an optician. Giorgio also started to collect old glasses and has filled his shop with old wooden storage systems and display cabinets and frames that hold eighteenth-, nineteenth– and

Foto Veneta Ottica

LOOKING GOOD IS A SERIOUS AFFAIR

Milan has a lot to offer on the shopping front. The 'bella figura', or the 'beautiful figure', runs deep within Italian culture. Clothes matter, appearance matters, and when you meet someone, you can be pretty sure that they're taking careful note of what you're wearing, including your shoes. It's this culture of image and of beauty that's at the heart of Italian society. Italians love to look good, and for the Milanese, this all matters in their own distinctive, understated key. That coat might be expensive, but it could one day become an heirloom for a daughter or granddaughter, and there is always the question of prestige.

twentieth-century models that include pince-nez, monocles and lorgnettes. Giorgio's son Emanuele chooses modern frames from independent brands that cannot be found elsewhere. There's a large selection of vintage, alongside the new frames on offer, along with end of line stock. Choose from the latest models, find that perfect pair of 1970s acetate glasses or be bold in a pair of 1950s butterfly sunglasses. There's something to suit every pocket, and it's popular with the fashion world, for obvious reasons.

Foto Veneta Ottica, Via Torino, 57, 02 805 5735, Mon–Sat 10 am – 1.30 pm; 2.30 – 7.00 pm. **www.fotovenetaottica.com**

WHEN STYLE IS A QUESTION OF MILANESE WOMEN

If you want to learn a thing or two about fashion while you're in Milan, look at the women. These Milanese women know style and understand beauty. In the past, the Milanese 'signora' was born into one of the best Milanese families, raised in Milan, and dressed in elegant suits or 'tailleurs', as she would call them from the French, complete with gloves and the highest quality accessories. Her clothes may not have always been couture, but were still made by a trusted 'sarta', a dressmaker who made extremely high quality clothing both in terms of craftsmanship and the materials used. This Milanese signora was wealthy, fashionable in a discreet and understated way, and knew all the right people, whether through her connections with the old Milanese aristocratic families, or with the worlds of industry or politics. She transferred this sense of discreet style to every area of her life, including her home and the way her children dressed. This was a time when clothes were chosen according to the occasion and the time of day, of cocktail dresses and evening gowns. What she wore to the opening night of La Scala was always a matter of serious business. The 'signora milanese' is sometimes known as 'sciura', Milanese dialect for signora,

and pronounced more like 'shiura', although to say someone is a 'sciura' can also be used as a criticism of over-conservative dress sense. In her most glamorous form, she's found fame on Instagram @sciuraglam, and sciura has become a byword for Milanese glamour.

Her daughters and granddaughters continue the form in twenty-first century key. They may not necessarily be Milanese-born but have chosen to make Milan their home, and fully understand that Milanese living is always a question of style. The style that's found in their wardrobes and homes may have embraced vintage, maximalism, ethnic and other influences to create a more eclectic mix. Yet it all still retains a certain 'milanesità', that attention to quality and beauty that marks it out as Milanese. Sit, study and take note, and when in doubt, less is always more. You will see women wearing more, but they know exactly how to carry it; don't risk verging on the vulgar. A word about designer labels. Milanese women might be wearing designer labels but they won't generally show you they are. Milan is not the city for walking around head to toe in labels.

Finally, remember your sunglasses, designer if you can.

SANT'AMBROGIO/ CORSO MAGENTA

Boutique and design shopping in the heartland of Leonardo da Vinci's Milan

M1 Cordusio, M1 Conciliazione; number 16 tram from the centre

Sant'Ambrogio and Corso Magenta, with their links to Leonardo da Vinci and his time in Milan, is one of the city's loveliest neighbourhoods. This is the Milan of Leonardo da Vinci, when he first came here from Florence and lived at the Sforza Castle at the court of Ludovico Sforza and his young wife Beatrice d'Este. Just like the area known as the Golden Quad today, Corso Magenta was once home to churches and monasteries.

During medieval times it was known as 'Borgo delle Grazie', a reference to the Basilica di Santa Maria delle Grazie that you'll find there. During the Renaissance, the Milanese dukes invested in churches and the arts, just as other families were doing so in other Italian cities such as Florence and Mantua. Ludovico Sforza commissioned work on the basilica and turned it into the family mausoleum, although sadly the first to be buried there was Beatrice herself, who died in childbirth. He also commissioned Leonardo da Vinci to paint *The Last Supper*, Milan's most famous work of art, on the the walls of the refectory nearby. It's this expression of beauty that you find all over the city, the thread that brings it all together. This same love of beauty underpins everything you see, from fashion to Renaissance art to churches and palazzos.

In the nineteenth and twentieth centuries, the area became the heart of bourgeois Milan, where rich industrialists built beautiful villas concealing exquisite courtyards and homes. Corso Magenta is one of Milan's loveliest streets. It still has some historic shops and a church named San Maurizio al Monastero Maggiore, once the city's most important monastery, which is often known as Milan's Sistine Chapel. For

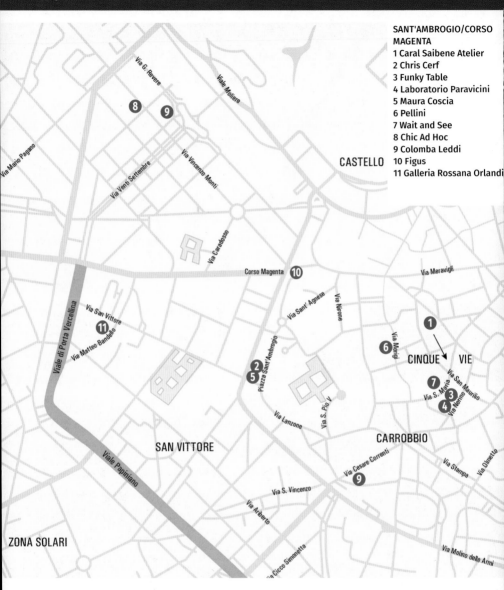

SANT'AMBROGIO/CORSO
MAGENTA
1 Caral Saibene Atelier
2 Chris Cerf
3 Funky Table
4 Laboratorio Paravicini
5 Maura Coscia
6 Pellini
7 Wait and See
8 Chic Ad Hoc
9 Colomba Leddi
10 Figus
11 Galleria Rossana Orlandi

shopping, Corso Vercelli offers high street names, although the area around Piazza Wagner has some lovely finds. All should be savoured slowly.

The area known as Sant'Ambrogio has the 5 Vie design district. The 5 Vie are, literally, five streets: Via Santa Marta, Via Santa Maria Podone, Via

Santa Maria Fulcorina, Via Bocchetto and Via del Bollo. Together they promote design within the area. The whole area comes to life during Milan's Design Week as part of the city's Fuorisalone programme, which holds events all around Milan. The main event during Design Week is the Salone Internazionale del Mobile (International Furniture Fair), and the Fuorisalone programme are events that take place 'fuori salone', or outside the fair, and throughout the city.

EAT AND DRINK

COFFEE

Pasticceria Marchesi

This is your Milanese café of once upon a time. Go for Sacher cake, the most exquisite pastel-coloured fondant cakes and pralines. Also look out for their panettones and veneziana cakes. Made all year round, they're held to be some of the very best.

Pasticceria Marchesi, Via Santa Maria alla Porta, 11a, 02 876730, Tues–Sat 7.30 am – 8 pm, Sunday 8.30 am – 1 pm. **www.pasticceriamarchesi.com**

LUNCH

Cavoli a Merenda

What in Italian we'd call 'una chicca', or 'an absolute treat'. Located in a beautiful eighteenth-century palazzo with a terrace, this is the restaurant of the cooking school of the same name.

The menu is Italian and changes every week according to the season. In the afternoons, they serve coffee, tea, cake and homemade ice creams. Book in advance as it's quite small, which merely adds to the appeal.

Cavoli a Merenda, Corso Magenta, 66, 335 467 9513, Mon–Fri 12.30 – 2.30 pm. **www.cavoliamerenda.eu**

APERITIVO

B Café

Soak up the vintage atmosphere and enjoy panini, cocktails and traditional taglieri or plates of Italian cold meats and cheese.

B Café, Via San Maurilio, 20, 02 8909 3317, Mon-Thurs 8 am – 1 am, Fri 8 am – 2 am, Sat 10.30 am – 2 am. Instagram and Facebook @Bcafe20

DINNER

La Brisa

Popular with the fashion set, La Brisa serves seasonal Italian food and has a lovely internal garden for warmer months.

La Brisa, Via Brisa, 15, 02 8645 0521, Mon–Sun 12.45 – 2.30 pm, 7.45 – 10.30 pm. **www.ristorantelabrisa.it**

Bistro Aimo e Nadia

Bistro Aimo e Nadia is a venture between gallery owner Rosanna Orlandi and the owners of Michelin starred Milan restaurant Il Luogo di Aimo e Nadia, with a textile partnership with Etro. The result is a maximalist design testament to Rosanna Orlandi's style: eclectic, and which prioritises both established and emerging designers. It's popular with creative types, and a hotspot during Fashion Week.

Bistro Aimo e Nadia, Via Matteo Bandello, 14, 02 4802 6205, Mon–Sat 7 am – 11 pm. **www.bistrotaimoenadia.com**

Trattoria Milanese

Trattoria Milanese is a local favourite that's been serving traditional cooking since 1933. Go for basic staples risotto alla Milanese (saffron risotto) or risotto al salto, the same saffron risotto which is then fried.

Trattoria Milanese, Via Santa Marta, 11, 02 8645 1991 Mon–Sat 12 – 3pm, 7 – 10.45 pm. Facebook @TrattoriaMilanese1933

CULTURE STOP

Basilica di Sant'Ambrogio

This beautiful Lombard Romanesque church is where Sant'Ambrogio (Saint Ambrose), the patron saint of Milan, founded his church in AD 379 and is now buried in the crypt here.

Basilica di Sant'Ambrogio, Piazza Sant'Ambrogio, 15. Visiting hours for tourists are as follows: Mon–Sat 10 am – 12.30 pm, 2.30 – 6 pm; Sun 3 pm – 5 pm.

Chiesa di San Maurizio al Monastero Maggiore

Take a break and soak up the beautiful frescoes at this early sixteenth-century street-side church that was once attached to Milan's most important Benedectine monastery.

Chiesa di San Maurizio al Monastero Maggiore, Corso Magenta, 15, open Tues–Sun 9.30 am – 7.30 pm.

Vigna di Leonardo

The 'Vigna di Leonardo' or 'Leonardo's

Vineyard' is the vineyard that Ludovico Sforza gave to Leonardo da Vinci in 1498. Casa degli Atellani is the adjoining house given by Ludovico Sforza to the Atellani family. It was restructured by Piero Portaluppi in the 1920s, and various original frescoes were revealed. The vineyard was replanted according to various scientific studies thanks to the Fondazione Portaluppi and the present owners of the house, and re-opened for Expo 2015.

La Vigna di Leonardo' (Leonardo's Vineyard), Corso Magenta, 65, 02 4816150, Mon–Sun 9 am – 6 pm. (Do check their website for occasional days when the vineyard is closed.) Joint tickets are available for both Leonardo's Vineyard and *The Last Supper*.
www.vignadileonardo.com

The Last Supper

Book in advance to visit Leonardo Da Vinci's last fifteenth-century masterpiece *The Last Supper*. It's preserved at the Basilica di Santa Maria delle Grazie. It's Milan's most famous work of art and shows Christ and his disciples right at the moment when Christ says he knows one of them has betrayed him. You have to book to visit because of the fragility of the work, entry is allowed every fifteen minutes with a maximum capacity of thirty people at any given time.

The Last Supper, Chiesa di Santa Maria delle Grazie, Piazza di Santa Maria delle Grazie, Tuesday to Sunday 8:15 am – 7 pm (last

Adobe Stock

The Basilica di Santa Maria delle Grazie where Leonardo's 'The Last Supper' is preserved.

Adobe Stock

entrance 6.45 pm), price €10 (+ €2 reservation fee). Tickets can be purchased by contacting the call centre (toll number, Mon–Sat 8 am – 6.30 pm) on: +39 02 92800360 or online on the official website: www.cenacolovinciano.org. Tickets are also available through some tour operators that offer city tours or guided visits to the Last Supper. Prices may vary from €45 to €100. Useful links include:
www.zaniviaggi.com;
www.autostradaleviaggi.com;
www.viator.com;
www.getyourguide.com;
www.musement.com; www.tickitaly.com

SANT'AMBROGIO AND THE 5 VIE

Centre of design, art and artisan workshops, the 5 Vie Design District showcases Made in Italy during Milan's yearly Design Week. This is upmarket shopping in exquisite boutiques and places that are passed on by word-of-mouth, alongside beautifully kept palazzos. Just wander those streets and enjoy.

Carla Saibene Atelier (womenswear)

Carla Saibene's eclectic taste mixes attention to detail and quality fabrics alongside a carefully selected range of accessories, shoes, jewellery and handmade ceramics. The fit of her trousers is said to flatter any woman and any shape. Her clothes are sold exclusively in Italy at her atelier in Milan.

Carla Sailbene Atelier, Via San Maurilio, 20, 02 874008, Mon 3.30 – 7.30 pm, Tues–Sat 10.30 am – 2 pm, 3–7.30 pm, Instagram @carlasaibene

Chris Cerf (womenswear)

Christiane Cerf designs beachwear and clothes for the city in a beautiful palazzo in Piazza Sant'Ambrogio. Do note that the shop isn't accessible from the street. To get in you need to go through the gates, turn right and go up to the door on the left. Contrary to what you may feel, it isn't appointment only. Many people come to the piazza to see the famous Chiesa di Sant'Ambrogio, and just call in to have a look. Christiane

Dress by Chris Cerf. Renzo Alberganti

arrived in Milan from Brazil as a young woman in the early 1980s, when she began her career as a swimwear designer. Years of experience followed at the head of her family's large swimwear companies Okay Brasil and Cores do Sol. Nowadays she's still putting her energies into designing swimwear, inspired by her travels in Brazil, Kenya and most recently India. Her crocheted bikinis are striking, plain-coloured bikinis with contrasting coloured crochet, and the Brazilian influence is evident in her clothes through her use of colour, particularly yellow, and vibrant prints.

Christiane uses two methods of printing: digital and hand-block printing. The latter is done in India, using wooden blocks that are dipped in paint and stamped by hand onto the fabric. Christiane produces the design, it is then transformed into a wooden block, and this basic design is then repeated in a series to make up the overall design. Vegetable colours are used to bring silk and cotton fabrics to life, which are then made into dresses, shirts and scarves that bring a colourful injection to city life. And of course, swimwear and beach robes, as this is where Christiane began, and the area to which she always returns. The result is unique, a glorious celebration of culture and colour in the heart of one of the most quintessentially Milanese squares in Milan. The shop also takes part in Design Week as part of Milan's Fuorisalone and regularly hosts designers and organises events at the shop.

Chris Cerf, Piazza Sant'Ambrogio, 16, 335 617 5013, Tues–Sat 10 am – 1.30 pm, 3–7 pm.
www.chriscerf.com

Funky Table (homewear and accessories)

Funky Table sells tableware and other homeware. Sisters Mariangela and Titti Negroni opened the shop after various years in the world of fashion and design. The look is a delicious feast of colour: a mix of ceramics, textiles, ornamental objects and more from China, India, Portugal, Africa, the UK and Italy. If you're here at Christmas, don't forget to pick up some fairy lights and retro baubles.

Funky Table, Via Santa Marta, 19, 02 3674 8619, Mon 3 – 7 pm, Tues–Sat 10 am – 7pm.
www.funkytable.it

Laboratorio Paravicini (ceramics)

Costanza Paravicini started making ceramics more than twenty years ago, which are distinctive for their hand-painted decorations and use of pattern. Go for exquisite dinner services, tea and coffee sets and more which are hand-made right before your eyes, using rare techniques that give beautiful results. Each year Costanza's daughters Benedetta and Margherita design a new collection that is presented during Design Week.

Laboratorio Paravicini, Via Nerino, 8, 02 7202 1006, Mon–Fri 9 am – 6.30 pm.
www.parravicini.it

Maura Coscia (accessories)

Maura Coscia makes exclusive handmade bags from brocades, velvets and other materials to create a product that is not only beautiful, but functional

Maura Coscia. Amanda Naudi

too. After her studies at the Academy of Fine Arts of Brera, she later came to fashion almost by accident. She showed her first collection of bags in 2007, opened her first shop in 2010, and has been here in Piazza Sant'Ambrogio since 2016. Her bags are generally classic in shape, and use brightly coloured fabrics, stripes and paisleys that bring them to life. Maura also works with clients to make bags upon request.

Maura Coscia, Piazza Sant'Ambrogio, 16, 328 2140059, Tues–Sat 10.30 am – 7 pm, also by appointment throughout the week. **www. mauracoscia.it**

Pellini (jewellery)

The history of Pellini reads like a textbook example of how craft traditions are passed down through a family business. In this case there are three women. The first is Emma Caimi Pellini (the grandmother of the family), who studied at the Accademia di Belle Arti di Brera, the prestigious fine arts' academy in Brera. In 1950 she won second and third prize in the category 'imitazione del gioello' – literally, 'imitation of the jewel' – at the Triennale Design Exhibition. In 1951 she was invited to show her work in Saks Fifth Avenue in New York. The second is daughter Carla, who took over in the 1960s in Palazzo Belgioioso, and the third her daughter, Donatella, who followed in the 1980s. Donatella brought her contemporary vision to the atelier, worked with French and Italian fashion designers during the 1990s and became known for her work with resin. Her work fuses modern techniques with artisan craftsmanship and is a vibrant kaleidoscope of colour and more subtle pieces.

Her collection of semi-precious stones was launched in 2000. This is the original shop in the eighteenth-century Palazzo Belgioioso, where a collection of the company's jewellery dating from the 1950s is also held. There are two other shops at Via Manzoni, 20, and Corso Magenta, 11. The shop in Via Manzoni specialises in unique pieces made from semi-precious stones, while the shop at Corso Magenta has work by other artisans and artists which changes every month.

Pellini, Via Morigi, 9 , 02 7201 0213, Mon–Fri 9.30 am – 7.30 pm, Via Manzoni, 20, 02 7600 8084, Mon 3 – 7.30 pm, Tues–Sat 10 am – 7.30 pm, 02 7201 0569, Mon 3 – 7.30 pm, Tues–Sat 10 am – 7.30 pm. **www.pellini.it**

Wait and See (womenswear)

Uberta Zambeletti worked for various fashion houses and gained a wealth of experience as a stylist, interior decorator, art director and fashion coordinator before she opened her shop Wait and See in an eighteenth-century convent in Milan's historical city centre. She mixes

Wait and See

Wait and See

niche brands and a selection of vintage pieces according to a philosophy of 'la vita è bella' – 'life is beautiful' – and looking at the visual merchandising in the shop, this certainly appears to be true. There are clothes, shoes, bags, jewellery and various other objects, from childhood sweets to cushions and stationery, that will make you want to fill your suitcase. Pieces are sourced from all over the world and the shop has a distinct feel of bohemian, with a pinch of glam all rolled into one.

Wait and See, Via Santa Marta, 14, 02 7208 0195, Mon 3.30 – 7.30 pm, Tues–Sat 10.30 am – 7.30 pm.
 www.waitandsee.it

ALSO VISIT...
Stylist Susanna Ausoni's **My Room** mixes vintage clothing with new. The shop is inspired by her grandmother's closet and the knowledge that you can put old with new and make a look happen. The style at **Suede** is slightly French, slightly vintage and always elegant. They have their own brand, Volver, that's sold internationally, through which they produce clothes, shoes, bags and bijoux. They also sell other brands that may change according to the season, all made in Italy.

My Room Vintage shop, Via San Maurilio, 24, 02 8970 8061, Mon 3.30 – 7.30 pm, Tues–Sat 11.30 am – 7.30 pm. **www.myroomshop.com**

Suede, Via Cesare Correnti, 21, 02 5811 8308, Mon 3.30 – 7.30 pm, Tues–Sat 10 am – 7.30 pm. **www.suede.it**

CORSO MAGENTA

Walk along here when it's getting dark on a cold winter's evening as the sky takes on the blue tones of dusk and an orange Carrelli tram travels down the street. This is the Milan of the old bourgeoisie, a Milan that sprang up at the end of the nineteenth century in what were originally agricultural fields. You'll find some beautiful palazzos, including the Italian Liberty Style Casa Laugier at Corso Magenta, 96. Fashion-wise, watch and take note. Go to a café and just sit. If you're looking for a lesson in understated chic, you'll find it here.

Chic ad hoc (jewellery and accessories)

The story of Chic ad hoc takes us back to the years of the 1930s before Milan's Golden Quad existed, and it was home of the Milanese upper classes and aristocracy. A shop named Al Gingillo started making and selling new jewellery fashioned after the styles in Paris, or bijoux as it was known. It became the jewellery loved and worn by Milanese ladies at Teatro alla Scala and other society events. Eighty years later, the shop moved to Via Monti and Chic ad hoc opened. They have a gorgeous selection of costume jewellery including thirties-style pieces and more contemporary ones, and accessories such as bags. Check out their 1930s style pochettes and sunglasses.

Chic ad hoc, Via Vincenzo Monti, 47, 02 8457 4929, Mon 3 – 7 pm, Tues–Sat 10 am – 2 pm, 3 – 7 pm. www.chicandhoc.com

Colomba Leddi (women's clothing and home furnishings)

Colomba Leddi worked with many important fashion designers until 1996 when she opened her own atelier. She's also worked as a costume designer for theatre and film productions, her prints have been displayed at the Triennale Art and Design Museum and she is course leader and teaches on the BA Fashion Design at the Accademia di Belle Arti in Milan. She draws her inspiration from what she sees in the natural world to create unique pieces that are transformed into an item of clothing or something for the home. She experiments with printing techniques such as ink-jet printing, and with different fabrics such as chiffon, cotton and nylon. All items are made in Italy, and her pieces are also sold in important boutiques in Italy and internationally, such as Egg and The Cross in London.

Colomba Leddi, Via Revere, 3, Ring 02 4801 4146 or 02 3668 4944 to make an appointment. www.colombaleddi.it

Figus Designer

If you 're looking for traditional craftsmanship combined with quality, attention to detail with an eye firmly on the future, Figus Designer is not just

Courtesy of Figus Designer

made in Italy, but made in Milan. They've been producing quality handmade bags, shoes, accessories and handmade jewellery at accessible prices since 1979, when Giorgio Figus set up the company. Daughter Eleonora, who is the company's designer today, grew up amid the world of the company's shops and the workshop – its colours and smells and shapes of leather, and it was all this that would eventually influence her own work as a designer. Eleonora's design vision unites a belief in artisan craftsmanship as a way of conserving both history and culture with new and innovative ways of doing so. Her designs combine colour,

Courtesy of Figus Designer

design, function, a personal touch and a love of detail, and all at accessible prices.

Her jewellery collection 'Figus Satin' was inspired by ancient Etruscan jewels and the contrasts between the materials used. In 2013-2014 Eleonora's Wi-figus Bag was displayed at the Triennale Art and Design Museum following the 2013 design Competition 'A Designer for companies'. The bag was designed according to everyday needs, so with a pocket for a notebook, one for a tablet, and a system to quickly recharge your mobile phone within the internal lining. The bag was greatly acclaimed, was shown during Milan's Design Week and at Expo Gate 2015, along with fifteen other design projects, where it won. Bags are made in both leather and 100 per cent vegan ecopelle. Also visit their shop on Corso Garibaldi where they have their workshop. They're happy to organise guided tours, so if you're interested in artisan craftsmanship and would like to learn more, send them an email to info.figusdesigner@gmail.com

Figus, Corso Magenta, 31, 02 8645 0155 Mon 3 – 7 pm, Tues–Thurs 10.30 am – 2 pm, 3 – 7.30 pm, Fri–Sat 10.30 am – 7pm; Corso Garibaldi, 46, Mon 3 – 7.30 pm, Tues–Sat 10 am – 7.30 pm. **www.figusdesigner.com**

Galleria Rossana Orlandi (design and homeware)

Rossana Orlandi worked as a knitwear designer and then opened her store in 2002 in what used to be a tie factory, and realised a long time passion for

design. The result is an eclectic dialogue of vintage and contemporary design, furniture and art. International names, new designers, collections and one-offs, all create a place of treasures that is one of Milan's most celebrated stores. Rossana Orlandi herself is an Italian style icon, known for her sense of dress and her statement eyewear. She began as a spin yarn consultant for Giorgio Armani and Donna Karan and is now considered one of the grand

Galleria Rossana Orlandi. Galleria Rossana Orlandi

Galleria Rossana Orlandi

dames of the design world. Orlandi is a must-visit on any Design Week itinerary when it's estimated that about 55,000 visitors pass through. The carefully curated selection of designers and the collaborations that take place are often way ahead of trend.

Galleria Rossana Orlandi, Via Matteo Bandello, 14/16 02 4674471, Mon–Sat 10 am – 7 pm. **www.rosannaorlandi.com**

ALSO VISIT...
The women's clothing at **Angela Orsolani** is sophisticated, original and contemporary. At **Monica G**, every piece by Monica Galletto is unique. She spends her time between India and Italy and the inspiration from both is evident in her work.

Angela Orsolani, Via Vincenzo Monti, 32, 02 4801 9554, Mon 3 – 7.30 pm, Tues–Sat 10 am – 7.30 pm. Instagram and Facebook @angelaorsolani

Monica G Gioelli, Via Brisa, 15, 333 864 1216 Mon–Sat 11 am – 3 pm, 4 – 7 pm. Instagram @ilovemyjaipur

CITYLIFE SHOPPING DISTRICT
M5 Tre Torri

CityLife was built on the site of the old Fiera Milano that was used to hold trade fairs, conferences and exhibitions. It's a new shopping, business and residential district, a car-free area with advanced energy systems. The complex is distinctive for its architecture, such as its 209-metre Allianz Tower by architects Arata Isozaki and Andrea Maffei, while the Generali Tower by Zaha Hadid is the twisted tower with forty-four floors. The third tower, the Libeskind, was designed by Daniel Libeskind and draws upon the Renaissance cupola as it moves concavely towards what's known as its crown above. Mario Bellini's shining Comet is the huge structure that covers or embraces the new Milano Convention Centre, the largest convention centre in Europe. The Comet lights itself at dawn and sunset with the natural light, and is lit up at night.

The CityLife Shopping District, designed by Zaha Hadid who also designed the MAXXI museum, Rome's National Museum of 21st Century Art, is Italy's largest shopping district

with 100 shops which cover fashion, technology, cosmetics, design and restaurants, and a multiplex cinema. Expect lots of high street names. There's also a food hall, the Anteo CityLife cinema, and a huge urban park, the city's second largest, complete with vegetable gardens. Check out their website at **www.citylifeshoppingdistrict.it**

MILANESE CAFÉ CULTURE IS A GLORIOUS ART FORM

Breakfast at the bar, as cafés are known around here, is the most Italian of experiences, and particularly when you're in Milan. Sit down, or do as the Milanese do for a truly authentic experience. This means standing at the bar for a 'caffè', as an espresso is known, a 'macchiato caldo' or a cappuccino, with or without a brioche (go for with, it's the quintessential breakfast experience). The whole thing is quite a businesslike affair, but the charm of standing there, while smartly uniformed barmen busy themselves amid chatter and steam, is really quite intoxicating. Order at the till, pay, hand your receipt to one of the people behind the bar, drink your coffee, eat your brioche and begin your day. Sitting down can be considerably more expensive, especially in the more exclusive cafés so if you're on a budget, be warned. Breakfast is generally until around 11 am, after which you could always order an espresso and a couple of biscuits. And if you must order a cappuccino after lunch, bring an element of irony to the situation. You're the tourist who understands perfectly that this is not the done thing. You've just chosen not to care. Finally don't forget merenda. Not just an after-school snack for children, in its chicest form it involves small cakes known as pasticcini, works of art in their own right. It's similar to the British afternoon tea, with bignè and cannoncini, and delightful little fruit-topped tarts in shortcrust pastry casings that constitute one of Milan's greatest sweet experiences.

PORTA VENEZIA/ CORSO BUENOS AIRES
Elegant boulevards alongside high street shopping

M1 Porta Venezia

The initial stretch of Corso Venezia forms part of the Golden Quad, or the 'quadrilatero d'oro' in Italian, Milan's

luxury shopping district. After the fashion comes the silence, or rather the 'quadrilatero del silenzio' – the 'quad of

Building by Piero Portaluppi, Corso Venezia.

Adobe Stock

Casa Galimberti at via Malpighi, 3, is a beautiful example of Italian Liberty style architecture. Adobe Stock

silence,' that area between the Golden Quad and Porta Venezia. This is where you'll find Liberty villas, hidden gardens and statues, and where you can admire the flamingos in the garden of the private Villa Invernizzi at Via Cappuccini, 3, home of the cheese tycoon, Invernizzi. His wife Enrica was famous for her jewellery, particularly at the opening night of La Scala. Also look out for the Liberty-style Casa Galimberti at Via Marcello Marpighi, 3.

Amongst Milan's most elegant boulevards, Corso Venezia then leads along to Porta Venezia, one of Milan's city gates and the neighbourhood of the same name. Nearby are two of Milan's art galleries, Padiglione d'Arte Contemporanea (PAC) and the Galleria d'Arte Contemporanea (GAM). Corso Buenos Aires, leading off from the Porta Venezia gate, is almost 1½ km long and a high street shopping lover's paradise. You'll find plenty of high street names, alongside historic places such as De Bernardi that's been there since the early 1900s and is still selling underwear, gloves, scarves and a whole range of wedding underwear for the bride-to-be. The streets off Corso Buenos Aires, Milan's high-street mecca, form one of Milan's hubs for food and drink. It's beautiful, lively, multicultural, has some great LGBT bars, and is the home for Pride Square during Milano Pride that takes place every June. It also has some lovely gardens and if you fancy a quieter moment, head for the Parco Indro Montanelli to recharge before making your way back, just in time for aperitivo.

PORTA VENEZIA/CORSO BUENOS AIRES. 1 Ami Mops, 2 Atelier Bergnach, 3 Pause, 4 Sunnei Store, 5 Imarika.

EAT AND DRINK

BREAKFAST

Pavé

When Pavé opened in 2012, it pretty much turned the whole concept of the Milanese café on its head. This was different to many of the cafés found around Milan, more Nordic cool mixed with an element of being in your grandmother's kitchen. Come to Pavé for the pastries because really, these are pastries you will dream about long after. They also do cakes, soups, sandwiches, and aperitivo.

Pavé, Via Felice Casati, 27, 02 9439 2259, Tues–Fri 8 am – 9 pm, Sat–Sun 8.30 am – 7 pm. **www.pavemilano.com**

LUNCH

LùBar

Set in Milan's Neoclassical Villa Reale along with the city's Modern Art Gallery, this bistrot café is surrounded by greenery at every turn. Go for Sicilian street food such as arancini and panelle palermitane (fried chickpea flour fritters). Owners Lucrezia and Ludovico Bonnacorsi, son and daughter of fashion designer Luisa Beccari, started out in an Ape Car selling Sicilian arancini all over Italy. You'll find one positioned permanently in Milan's Central Station.

LùBar, Via Palestro, 16, 02 83 52 77 69, Mon–Sun 8 am – 12 am. **www.lubar.it** Central Station, Piazza Duca D'Aosta, 1, Mon–Sun 7 am – 9 pm.

APERITIVO

Champagne Socialist

Go for organically farmed raw wines and sourced Italian aperitivo.

Champagne Socialist, Via Lecco, 1, 02 204 7295, Mon–Sun. 6 – 12 pm. **www.socialist.wine**

Mint Garden Café

Owners Renato and Lucia added a bistrot to their florist's, and the result is green and lovely. Go for cocktails amid the flowers.

Mint Garden Café, Via Felice Casati, 12, 02 8341 7806, Mon 8 am – 11 pm, Tues 8am – 12 am, Wed–Thurs 8 am – 1 am, Sat 8.30 am – 1.30 am, Sun 8.30 am – 12 am. **www.mintgardencafe.it**

CULTURE STOP

Villa Necchi Campiglio

Take the short walk to Villa Necchi Campiglio, built between 1932 and 1935, with garden, swimming pool and tennis court. Designed by Italian architect Piero Portaluppi, it fuses Rationalist urban architecture with Art Deco interiors. It was built for sisters Nedda and Gigina Necchi. The Necchi Campiglio family, who mixed with the Milanese society and aristocratic circles of the time, were rich industrialists, bourgeois, cultured and famous for Necchi sewing machines. Villa Necchi Campiglio was used as the setting for Luca Guadagnino's 2009 film *I am Love* starring Tilda Swinton, as it encapsulated the understated luxury and attention to detail that characterised the Milanese upper classes. Diego della Valle has shown Tod collections here. They also sometimes hold exhibitions relating to design and fashion, so do check their website before you go. This is the place where you ideally want to be lounging around in vintage 1930s clothing next to the artistic masterpieces that make up the house's art collection. Go for lunch in the café that looks out onto the garden.

Villa Necchi Campiglio, Via Mozart, 14, 02 7634 0121, villa Wed–Sun and café Mon–Sun 10 am – 6 pm. (Booking is advised.) **www.casamuseomilano.it**

SHOPPING

Ami Mops (costume jewellery)

Valentina and Matteo continue the family business begun by Matteo's mother, Barbara, who originally started out in decorative arts in Milan's historic district of Lazzaretto during the 1990s and later moved into costume jewellery. The majority of their bijoux is made out of resin and often in a geometric and minimalist style. All components are made in Italy, apart from Bohemian crystals and pearls.

Ami Mops. Matteo Sozzo

Ami Mops, Via Alessandro Tadino, 3, 02 2941 9183, Tues–Fri 11 am – 2 pm, 3.30–7 pm, Sat 11 am – 1 pm, 3.30 – 7 pm. **www.amimops.com**

Atelier Bergnach (women's clothing)

Elena Bergnach has been making beautifully made individual skirts for the past fifteen years. She likes to use contrast through colour and pattern, to play with the shape of a skirt, how it fits to a woman's shape, and favours details

Atelier Bergnach. Massimo Forcato, courtesy of Atelier Bergnach

fashion. Carefully researched items from the world's four most important catwalks are presented alongside lesser-known quality brands. Also look out for their label Kalia (from the Ancient Greek meaning home which is produced in Lombardy using traditional Lombard artisan techniques. The philosophy here is that clothes should enable a person to shine. Follow their Instagram and Facebook pages for lessons in how to put it all together to create that cool Milanese style. Bevilaqua herself gives the perfect example.

Imarika, Via Giovanni Morelli, 1, 02 7600 5268, Mon 3 – 7.30 pm, Tues-Sat 9.30 am – 1.30 pm, 3 – 7.30 pm, www.imarika.com

such as pockets or buttons. Skirts are generally structured with clean lines, and she believes that this is what helps to create their effect. Elena presents various models of skirts inside the atelier, which can be bought in sizes or sartorially made to measure. To complete the look, she proposes sartorial tops, blouses, bustiers and jackets.

Atelier Bergnach, Via Alessandro Tadino, 15, 02 8739 0327 / 3518033126, Tues–Sat 10 am – 1 pm, 3 – 7.30 pm **www.atelierbergnach.com**, Instagram @bergnach_skirt, Facebook @ bergnach_skirt

Imarika (womenswear)

Imarika is one of Milan's historic boutiques. It opened in Via Giovanni Morelli in 1979 and since then owner Benedetta Bevilaqua has been providing Milanese ladies and their daughters with high quality boutique

Pause (fashion and food)

Pause mixes fashion with food. The fashion is vintage and contemporary clothing and accessories and includes individual pieces that are made in Italy, and international names. The food includes mostly vegetarian dishes such as homemade pasta, soups and cous cous and quinoa salads. Also come also for

Pause. Anna Ricca for Casamenu, courtesy of Pause

their aperitivo with cocktails and organic wines. They also organise occasional art and photography exhibitions.

Pause, Via Federico Ozanam, 7, 02 3952 8151, Mon-Wed 8am – 10 pm, Thurs–Fri 8 am – 12 am, Sat 10 – 12 am. **www.pausemilano.com**

Sunnei Store (menswear, womenswear)

Sunnei is the distinctly contemporary Milan-based brand of friends Loris Messina and Simone Rizzo that started on Instagram, and found success in the United States and in Asia, and in particular South Korea. They started off designing menswear, and launched their first womenswear collection for spring/ summer 2018, both of which are sold at their flagship store in Milan. This is their first flagship store, and their only one to date in Italy. Their design philosophy is focused upon a meeting of timelessness and innovation, a playful and sometimes ironic take on classic Italian tailoring and assumptions. The inspiration for the name came from a road trip in the US when they realised the name Sunnei would imitate the Italian way of pronouncing the word 'sunny'.

Sunnei Store, Via Vincenzo Vela, 8, 02 2951 1728, Tues–Sat 12–6 pm. www.sunnei.it

ALSO VISIT...

Capelleria Mutinelli is a historic shop that's been along Corso Buenos Aires since 1888. They sell hats and accessories. Also visit **Atelier Titã Bijoux**, where mother-and-daughter team Laura and Céline make the lightest of lace earrings in a range of colours and styles. Jewellery at Silvia Cascione's **ModWax** design and crafts store is created using the lost-wax technique.

Capelleria Mutinelli, Corso Buenos Aires, 5, 02 2952 3594, Mon 3–7.30 pm, Tues–Fri 10 am – 1 pm, 3 – 7.30 pm, Sat 10 am – 1.30 pm, 3 – 7.30 pm.
www.mutinellicapellimilano.com

Atelier Titã Bijoux, Via Melzo, 12, 02 2052 0004, Tues–Sat 10.30 am – 1 pm, 2.30 – 7 pm. Their flagship store is at Via Madonnina, 13 (Brera), Tues–Sat 10.30 am – 7.30 pm, Sun 11.30 am – 7 pm.
www.titabijoux.com

Modwax, Via Felice Casati, 26, 02 670 6236, Tues–Sat 11 am – 7 pm. Facebook @modwax.design.crafts

Sunnei Store. Sunnei Store.

6

PORTA NUOVA/ CORSO COMO/CORSO GARIBALDI
Shopping below the skyscrapers

M2, M5 Corso Garibaldi

This is the face of the new Milan that looks forward and embraces the future. Milan's Porta Nuova district is the result of the massive urban regeneration project, one of Europe's largest, which involved the area around the Porta Garibaldi station and that known as the Varesine, which was once home to the legendary fairground. Its focus is Piazza Gae Aulenti, named after the famous architect who made

Comune di Milano

PORTA NUOVA/COROSO COMO/CORSO GARIBALDI. 1 Co Co, 2 Lipstick Vintage, 3 Minuit, 4 Noriem, 5 10 Corso Como, 6 Cargo, 7 Chiara Ferragni, 8 Colmer Lab.

Milan her home, and the skyscrapers that surround it and make up one of Milan's central business districts have changed Milan's skyline. The Unicredit Tower here is the highest in Italy at 231 metres. Also take a look Michele De Lucchi's Unicredit Pavilion, and at the Bosco Verticale (Vertical Forest) designed by Stefano Boeri Architetti, which was awarded the prize for the Best Tall Building Worldwide in 2015. Made up of two residential towers of 80 and 120 metres each, it's home to 900 trees and over 2,000 plants and aims to help combat Milan's pollution levels. Parco Biblioteca degli Alberi or Library of Trees is the park there.

In contrast, Corso Garibaldi is another of those areas in the city where you can feel an older Milan. If you walk out of the centre along Corso Garibaldi towards the Porta Nuova area and its skyscraper skyline, you'll see the contrast between the old and new Milan and how they meet together so beautifully. Isola was the working-class district where the creatives moved in, bought shops, bars and restaurants to create a more edgy neighbourhood vibe and found their niche. For bars and restaurants in the Isola district, see the relevant Isola section.

EAT AND DRINK

Eataly

Housed in what used to be the Teatro Smeraldo theatre, Eataly gathers high quality producers under one roof where you can shop, eat, and take cookery and wine tasting classes.

Eataly, Piazza Venticinque Aprile, 10, 02 4949 7301, Mon–Sun 8.30 am – 12 am. **www.eataly.net**

COFFEE

Pandenus

Small, cosy bar that does great cappuccino and brioche, lunch and aperitivo. There are various Pandenus bars throughout Milan.

Pandenus, Largo La Foppa, 5, 02 6556 0824, Mon 7 am – 11 pm, Tues/Wed 7 am – 12 am, Thurs 7 am – 1 am, Fri 7 am – 2 am, Sat 8 am – 2 am, Sun 8 am – 11 pm. **www.pandenus.it** (See website for other locations.)

Princi

There are now five Princi bakeries and cafés in Milan, and this one is at beginning of Corso Garibaldi near Brera. Come for focaccia, pizza, cake, brioche for breakfasts, hot meals and freshly baked bread, right through to way past aperitivo hour. It can get busy at lunchtime, but that's all part of the atmosphere.

Princi, Largo La Foppa, 2, 02 659 9013, Mon/Tues/Wed 7 am – 10 pm, Thurs/Fri 7 am – 11 pm, Sat–Sun 8 am – 11 pm. **www.princi.com** (See website for other locations.)

APERITIVO

Bar Radetzky

Named after General Radetzky who fought off the insurrection of the Five Days of Milan, it's a Milanese institution that's always popular at any time of the day.

Bar Radetzky, Corso Garibaldi, 105, 02 657 2645 Sun/Mon 8 am – 1.30 am, Tues/Wed/Thurs/Fri 8 am – 2 am Sat / Sun 9 am – 2 am. **www.radetzky.it**

Octavius Bar at The Stage

The Stage restaurant is inside the Replay concept store, and the Octavius Bar is its cocktail bar with décor reminiscent of a cabin on a nineteenth-century liner. It has over 900 spirit labels and a reputation of being one of the best places around for cocktails.

Octavius Bar at The Stage, 02 6379 3539, Piazza Gae Aulenti 4, 1am last entrance. **www.replaythestage.com**

DINNER

Ristorante Berton

Famous Michelin star restaurant in the Porta Nuova run by award-winning chef André Berton. It offers a refined atmosphere and a culinary repertoire of revisited Italian tradition.

Ristorante Berton, via Mike Bongiorno, 13, 02 6707 5801, Mon – Sat lunch 12.30 – 3 pm, dinner 7.30 – 10.30 pm.
www.ristoranteberton.com

CORSO GARIBALDI

Corso Garibaldi stretches from Piazza XXV Aprile to Brera in the centre. Start at one end and work your way along. Look back towards the view of the street with the skyscrapers in the background, a view that captures both old and new Milan. The street's days are filled with the everyday goings on of a Milanese street; the evenings are when the aperitivo hour starts and the whole place fills up. Porta Garibaldi, once known as Porta Comasina to indicate the road to Como, is the city gate in Piazza XXV Aprile, which was designed by Giacomo Moraglia and built during the 1820s. It became known as Corso Garibaldi when Garibaldi famously entered the city via the gate after his victory against the Austrians at San Fermo in 1859.

Nearby is the city's Cimitero Monumentale in Piazzale Cimitero Monumentale, where Biki, Jole Veneziani and Rosa

Adobe Stock

Genoni are buried. Gianni Versace, Maria Mandelli (Krizia) and Franca Sozzani are all honoured in the Famedio or Temple of Fame, among others who have significantly contributed to the city.

SHOPPING

Co Co (women's clothing and accessories)

Just off Corso Garibaldi, you'll find Nicoletta Ceccolini's shop, Co Co

(pronounced Co Cò). Nicoletta is a costume designer and has designed costumes for all types of productions; in theatres such as Teatro Out Off and Teatro Franco Parenti in Milan, Teatro Petrarca in Arezzo, and for films by directors such as Alessandro Genovese. In 1995 she opened a space in previous premises along Via Giannone, which housed her collection of clothing and accessories dating from the early 1900s to the present day. It was from here that she rented out items to the world of film, theatre and television.

Nicoletta Ceccolini in her shop.
Adelina Cingolini

Then in 2006 she began to design her own collections to sell alongside pieces from her own personal vintage archive. Nicoletta produces two collections a year, artisan-made to the highest standards. Come for a wide range of tailor-made trousers, skirts, coats and more, all in carefully researched fabrics that Nicoletta sources herself, and shoes that include models made from cloth, leather and chamois. The shop's style reflects Nicoletta's own, and is a mix of Made in Italy design and vintage. Items range from the 1930s to more recent times, include clothes, bags, shoes, bijoux and hats, and important names such as Gucci, Chanel, Yves Saint Laurent, Marni and Missoni. There's also a rent-a-dress service, so whether you're into sequins, lace or chiffon, take a look for that special occasion, that night at La Scala, or simply because you're in Milan and it's all making you feel like dressing up and playing the part.

Co Co, Via Volta, 5, 02 2900 6562, Mon 3.30 pm – 7.30 pm, Tues–Sat 10.30 am – 7.30 pm. **www.cocomilano.it www.nicolettaceccolini.it**

Lipstick Vintage (vintage women's clothing and accessories)

Walk into Lipstick Vintage and it's not unusual to witness a fashion shoot in progress. They sell a huge variety of vintage clothing and accessories including Chanel brooches, Hermès scarves, Christian Louboutin and Manolo Blahnik shoes, and have had couture pieces by Andrea Odicini, Biki, Thierry Mugler, Yves Saint Laurent, Mila Schön,

Curiel and Fausta Sarli. They also have a large selection of women's headwear such as cloche hats and headpieces decorated with Swarovski jewels and feathers. There are two shops, one in Milan and one in Genoa, so if you're ever in Liguria you know where to go.

Lipstick Vintage, Corso Garibaldi, 79 02 6208 6165, Mon 3.30–7.30 pm, Tues–Sat 10.30 am – 1 pm, 3.30 – 7.30 pm. Instagram and Facebook @lipstickvintagemilano

Minuit (womenswear)

The look at Minuit is retro chic with a touch of the bohemian. Lucia Mezzanotte specialised in fashion design at Central Saint Martins, London, and set up Minuit in 2009. Collections focus on originality that gives space to personal interpretation, high quality materials and artisan details. The shop also sells a variety of international brands.

Minuit, Corso Garibaldi, 127, 02 3653 4181, 10.30 am – 2 pm, 3–7.30 pm every day. **www.minuitmilano.com**

Noriem (womenswear)

The emphasis at Noriem is on the quality of the fabric and the cut within a concept of east meets west. Soft shapes are mixed with sharp tailoring and pleating using quality materials including jacquards that mix the more traditional with the modern to stunning effect, and always with a certain element of surprise.

Noriem, Corso Garibaldi, 50, 02 8724 6145, Mon–Sat 10 am – 7.30 pm. **www.noriem.jp**

ALSO VISIT...
Check out **Farfalle** along Via Varese for colour and prints, with a predominantly 1970s and vintage feel. Before you leave, call in at the **Odilla** chocolate shop along Corso Garibaldi. They're from Turin and make the most exquisite gianduia chocolates. Always leave a space in your suitcase for chocolate.

Farfalle, Via Varese, 12, 02 8738 9994, Mon 3.30–7.30 pm, Tues–Sat 10.30 am – 7.30 pm. **www.farfallemilano.com**

Odilla, Corso Garibaldi, 02 7209 5719, Mon–Sat 8.30 am – 1pm, 3pm–7.30 pm. **www.odillachocolat.it**

CORSO COMO

In the 1980s, Corso Como was the centre of Milan's nightlife, a popular place for football players, models, celebrities and businessmen. This period was known as 'Milano da bere', literally 'Milan to drink', from an advert for Ramazzotti bitter. It was quickly picked up by journalists to refer to a time of fashion, celebrities and social mobility after the difficult years that had preceded it. It was a time of renaissance or rebirth for Milan. In a similar way, Milan recently underwent a different kind of renaissance, this time in architectural and cultural terms. The new face that the area presents now is one of sleek new skyscrapers that have transformed the city's skyline. Piazza XXV Aprile is the large square that links Corso Como with Corso Garibaldi.

10 CORSO COMO (concept store)

This concept store, bookshop and art gallery is an absolute must-visit. In 1990 former editor and journalist Carla Sozzani, sister to the late *Vogue* editor Franca Sozzani, and a fashion editor and publisher in her own right, opened Galleria Carla Sozzani here in what was a disused garage. Her first photography exhibition showed Louise Dahl-Wolfe and throughout the years Sozzani has continued to profile photography as an art form. A year later she added a store, bookshop and the Garden Café, and 10 Corso Como was born. Sozzani had intended to only open a gallery, but when she realised she missed fashion, she started selling pieces by the designers she loved and who were pushing fashion forward, such as Martin Margiela, Azzedine Alaïa, Comme des Garçons and Prada's first womenswear collection.

There are so many reasons to come to 10 Corso Como, the store that has become Milan's cult shopping destination. Since it opened, Sozzani has added a gallery, the 10 Corso Como Café (complete with bar lounge), Hotel 3 Rooms and Terrace Roof Garden,

10 Corso Como. 10 Corso Como

The bookshop at 10 Corso Como. 10 Corso Como

10 Corso Como Garden Café. 10 Corso Como

complete with view of César Pelli's Unicredit Tower. The NN (No Name) studio was also started in 1991, a clothing and lifestyle line to contrast with the excess that had been witnessed in the 1980s. 10 Corso Como was groundbreaking because it was the first concept store in Milan. Sozzani conceived it as a kind of living magazine. The store itself is white, the perfect backdrop for the goods on sale, what could be classed as a (living and evolving) work of art in itself. There are fashion names such as Comme des Garçons, Sacai, Alexander McQueen, Maison Margiela (including jewellery), MSGM, Richard Quinn, Gareth Pugh, Vetements, Raf Simons, Taakk, Junya Watanabe, Philip Treacy hats, Kris Ruhs jewellery and artwork and Fiorucci tees. (Ruhs also designed the distinctive black and white logo.) Visit a

design collection that includes gorgeous Gucci homeware, and don't forget to visit the bookshop for the latest books and magazines in fashion, art, design, photography, architecture and popular culture. Then head to the Garden Café, with its conservatory outside filled with plants and greenery. The 10 Corso Como outlet is five minutes away from the main store where you can pick up discounted items from past season collections, vintage pieces and Manolo Blahnik. Other concept stores may have followed, but 10 Corso Como still maintains its place at the head of Milanese fashion and design.

As you walk into the courtyard with all its greenery, remember to look back and up at the 'casa di ringhiera' behind you. This is typical Milanese housing, basically a large block of flats with a shared balcony running along each floor, and is part of the history of the social fabric of an older Milan. (Ringhiera means railing.)

10 Corso Como, Corso Como, 10, store and bookshop: 02 2900 2674; gallery, 02 653531, 10.30 am – 7.30 pm every day, except Wed and Thurs 10.30 am – 9.00 pm.

Garden Café, 10, Corso Como, Corso Como, 10, 02 2901 3581, 11.30 am – 12 am every day 10 Corso Como outlet, Via Tazzoli, 3, 02 2901 5130, 11 am – 7 pm every day. www.10corsocomo.com

ALSO VISIT...

If you fancy spending a morning here visiting 10 Corso Como and then taking in a few boutiques, Corso Como has a lovely selection. **Boule de Neige** stocks a wide range of men's and women's designers including Yohi Yamamoto, Y3, Issey Miyake and and Marni. The style at Florentine company **Midinette** is refined, feminine, retro, and all made in Italy. Go for tailored coats with attention to detail and beautifully tailored dresses. **Momonì** is rather like a retro French boudoir, with clothes that are equally elegant and feminine. They also sell various French brands alongside their own brands Momonì and Attic and Barn that favour a relaxed yet elegant look. If you're interested in things for the home, **High Tech** is set in what used to be the ink factories of Italian newspaper *Corriere della Sera* and sells a mix of fashion accessories, furniture, kitchen accessories, lifestyle goods and more. It's a lovely place, set within a courtyard, with rooms leading off here and there that will make you want to browse for hours.

Boule de Neige, Corso Como, 3, 02 6291 0777, Mon–Sat 10 am – 7.30 pm. Sun 10.30 am – 1 pm, 2.30 – 7.30 pm. **www.bouledeneige.it**

High Tech, Piazza XXV Aprile, 12, 02 6241 101, Mon 1.30–7.30 pm, Tues–Sun 10.30 am – 7.30 pm. **www.cargomilano.it**

Midinette, Corso Como, 11, www.midinette-shop.com Mon–Sun 10.30am – 8pm. **www.midinettedesign.com**

Momonì, Corso Como, 2, 02 6379 3466, Mon–Sat 10.30 am – 7.30 pm. Sun 10.30 am – 2 pm, 3 – 7.30 pm. **www.momoni.it**

PORTA NUOVA

Piazza Gae Aulenti is the stunning square at the base of the Unicredit skyscraper with its upmarket boutiques and *Egg* installation by Alberto Garutti. The square was designed by Argentinian architect Cesar Pelli together with landscape company Land, and is named after famous architect Gae Aulenti, who made Milan her home. The *Egg* installation is Garutti's first permanent public installation in the city, made up of twenty-three brass tubes that come from four different levels of the building. So if you put your ear close to one of the tubes and listen, you can hear the noises of the city from another part of the building, such as the parking floors. The idea is to place the passer-by in closer relation to the architectural space in which they find themselves. Not only is it a beautiful and sustainable space, but it's also a square that encourages people to gather there by its fountains and in its cafés and restaurants, the primary function of any city square.

Italian influencer and entrepreneur **Chiara Ferragnni** opened her store here in 2017. Ferragni started her fashion

Egg by Albeto Garutti in Piazza Gae Aulenti.

blog *The Blonde Salad* in 2009 and by 2017 Forbes declared her the most important fashion influencer in the world. In 2013 she set up her own Chiara Ferragni Collection, and various pop-up stores in places such as Selfridges in London and Bon Marché in Paris. Her label is now an extremely successful business that includes clothing, shoes and accessories. In April 2015 she became the first blogger to appear on a *Vogue* cover, that of *Spanish Vogue*, and has since appeared on many others. Check out her Instagram page to see how she does it, along with Italian rapper husband Fedez. The Colmar flagship store is also here.

Chiara Ferragni, Via Vincenzo Capelli, 5, 02 3657 3157, Mon–Sun 10.30 am – 7.30 pm. **www.chiaraferragnicollection.com**

Colmar Lab, Piazza Gae Aulenti, 6, 02 6347 1465, Mon–Sun 10 am – 8 pm. **www.colmar.it**

THE FASHION LOVER'S LIST: CHILDREN'S CLOTHING

In fashion journalist Maria Pezzi's memoirs recorded by Guido Vergani, Pezzi speaks of her Milanese childhood at the beginning of the last century. She recalls how children would meet with their nannies in Parco Sempione and while the children played, the nannies would compare the children's clothes. What they were wearing, the quality of the material and where it came from mattered. Nowadays well-dressed Milanese children are still wearing the latest designs, and some of the most beautifully made clothing that often gives a nod to tradition. Here are some addresses you should know.

1. **Amanita** Concept store with artisan made children's clothing and accessories in Isola Via Federico Confolanieri, 21, 389 525 3755, Mon–Sat 10.30 am – 7.30 pm. **www.amanitamilano.it**

2. **Bonpoint** Parisian Elegance and the most delightful baby clothes along Via Manzoni. Perfect for special occasions. Via Manzoni, 15, 02 8901 0023, Mon – Sat 10 am – 7 pm, Sun 11 am – 7 pm. **www.bonpoint.com**

3. **Gusella** Opened by Dino Gusella in 1932, this historic children's clothing and shoe shop boasted famous clientele such as Princess Grace of Monaco. Via della Spiga, 31, 02 7634 0778, Mon–Sat 10 am – 7 pm, Sun 11 am – 7 pm. **www.gusellamilano.it**

4. **Meroni Si'** Refined elegance in the heart of Brera. Via Madonnina, 10, 02 8057406, Mon 3 – 7 pm, Tues–Sat 10 am – 2 pm, 3 – 7 pm. **www.meronisimilano.it**

5. **Pupi Solari** Pupi Solari arrived in Milan from Genoa in the 1950s and opened a boutique for children. Womenswear and menswear followed, then in 2018, at the age of 91, she decided to focus on children's clothing once more. Come here to see the childrenswear choices of the legendary lady of fashion. Via Lorenzo Mascheroni, 12, 02 463325, Mon 3 – 7 pm, Tues–Sat 10 am – 7 pm. Facebook @ pupisolarisrl, Instagram @pupisolari

ISOLA
Shopping with a creative, neighbourhood feel

M2 Garibaldi, M5 Isola

Come to the Isola neighbourhood that lies north of the Porta Garibaldi railway station on market day and the atmosphere is very much that of your local neighbourhood. Locals who have lived here for years mingle with the young families who have moved in over recent years, and all with the skyscrapers of the Porta Nuova and the Varesine in the background.

Isola's roots belong to Milan's industrial past of workshops, small factories and social housing that began to develop from the middle of the nineteenth century. Before that it was part of the agricultural land that lay on Milan's doorstep. 'Isola' literally means 'island'. From the mid-nineteenth

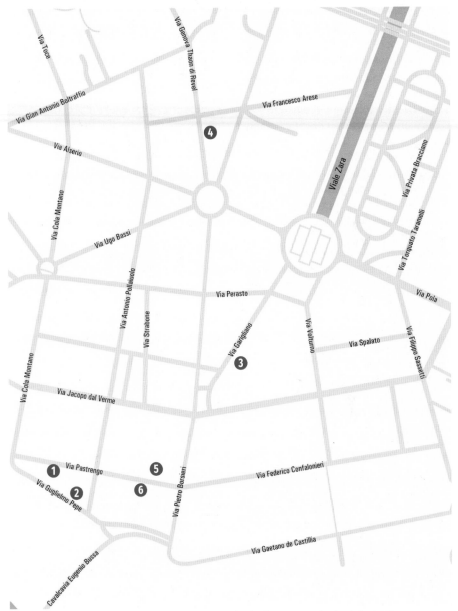

ISOLA. 1 Ambroeus, 2 Delphine Vintage, 3 Le Vintage, 4 Live in Vintage, 5 Monica Castiglioni, 6 Rapa.

century the area was separated from the rest of Milan by the Porta Garibaldi station. Isola was the area that lay between the railway tracks and Via Melchiorre Gioia, and up until the middle of the twentieth century, you had to cross a bridge to get to Corso Como and the rest of the city. The name also came from the particular type of housing called 'isole' that was there at the time, workshops and factories on the ground floors and housing on the floors above. In recent years an influx of creatives has arrived amid the traditional 'case di ringhiera', the characteristic housing with the shared wrought iron balconies running all along each floor; and brought art and design studios, boutiques, vintage shops, bars and restaurants.

Isola is also an official Design Week district that hosts young designers and emerging brands, while the Milan Design Market showcases new design talent as part of the Design Week Fuorisalone programme. Check out the street art around Isola along the underpass leading from Porta Garibaldi station, and along Via Carmagnola, Via Antonio Pollaiuolo and Via Angelo della Pergola and Piazza Fiddle. And don't forget the market in Piazza Tito Minitti that takes place every Tuesday, 7 am – 2 pm, and on Saturdays, 7 am – 5 pm. It's the perfect time to browse the stalls and check out some of the independent boutiques in the area. Creative, innovative, retro, vintage, and often eco-friendly, with a lively bar and restaurant scene to match: this is Isola.

EAT AND DRINK

LUNCH

Casa Ramen

People start queueing outside before it opens, so get there early as they don't take bookings. Reputed by many to serve some of the best ramen in town, this tiny restaurant with its shared tables offers some of Milan's best Japanese food, mainly steaming bowls of ramen. Try nearby Casa Ramen Super if you can't get a place.

Casa Ramen, Via Luigi Porro Lambertenghi, 25, 02 3944 4560, Tues–Sat 12.30 – 3 pm, 7.30 – 11.30 pm; Casa Ramen Super, Via Ugo Bassi, 26, 02 8352 9210, Tues–Fri 7.30 – 11 pm, Sat 12.30 – 3pm, 7.30 – 11 pm. **www.casaramen.it**

APERITIVO

Frida

Frida is an Isola favourite for cocktails and live music with a large courtyard for the warmer months. They also hold Frida Market and Let's Vintage. See their Facebook page for dates: @fridaisolamilano

Frida, Via Antonio Pollaiuolo, 3, 02 680260, Mon–Fri 12–3 pm, 6 pm – 2 am, Sat 12 pm – 2 am, Sun 5 pm – 1 am. **www.fridaisola.it**

The Botanical Club

There are three Botanical Clubs in Milan, all of which are always popular during fashion and design weeks. In Isola they have their own gin micro distillery and serve vegan and raw lunches. 2019 saw a new restaurant in Porta Venezia, and they have another bar on Via Tortona. (See page 172)

The Botanical Club, Isola: Via Pastrengo, 11, 02 3652 3846, Lunch Mon–Fri 12.30–2.30pm (Sat and Sun closed), dinner Mon–Sat 6.30–10.30 pm (Sun closed). Bar open Mon–Sat until 2 am. **www.thebotanicalclub.com**

DINNER

Deus ex Machina

Biker and surf haven, Deus ex Machina is the Australian company that unites the three worlds of motorbike, surfboard and cycle production with a clothing and accessories line. It has its own café, the Deus Café, open from breakfast (go for brunch) until late.

Deus ex Machina, Via Thaon di Revel, 3, 02 83 43 92 30, Sun-Thurs 9.30 am – 1 am, Fri–Sat 9.30 am – 2 am. **deuscustoms.com**

LIVE MUSIC

The Blue Note

Isola is also home to the Blue Note jazz club, the only European venue of the legendary New York jazz club. It's famous on the international jazz scene, and regularly hosts big names.

The Blue Note, Via Pietro Borsieri, 37, For information and tickets, call 02 6901 6888 Mon 12-7 pm, Tues - Sat 2-10pm. **www.bluenotemilano.com**

SHOPPING

Ambroeus (men's and women's vintage and second hand clothing and accessories)

Brother and sister Giorgia and Ettore Dell'Orto and their friend Massimo Miliani opened in Isola precisely because they felt it was the right environment in which to open a vintage and second-hand shop. That was in 2015,

Rachael Martin

and just a year later the *New York Times* ran an article of five places to visit in Isola, Milan, including Ambroeus. It put both Isola and Ambroeus on the international map, and with the use of social media they were able to access a far wider audience, and now send items regularly all around the world. Giorgia had previously worked in a second-hand shop in Notting Hill, London, and it was this experience that she brought to their shop in Milan. Giorgia, Ettore and Massimo see vintage and second-hand clothing as a considered ethical choice, and their emphasis is upon a reinterpretation of vintage within a contemporary context.

So you may find iconic Equipment silk shirts next to Yohji Yamamoto coats for men, 1980s Krizia jumpers next to Levi's 501s, Yves Saint Laurent skirts and made to measure 1960's dresses that sit by items from Gap and Max and Co. Running through this is a love of music that may reflect itself in a Bowie mood just as easily as a look inspired by Alison Mosshart. Go there and take a look for yourself. You may well chance on pieces by Maison Margiela, Alexander McQueen, Prada, Pucci and Gucci. Check out their Instagram account for their daily look that shows

MY MILAN: GIORGIA DELL'ORTO

'I start off in Isola where I live with breakfast at Cherry Pit or I'll pick up a focaccia at Panificio da Angela. Then I come to the shop to check everything's okay, then set off and walk along Corso Como and Corso Garibaldi towards the centre. One shop I like is Midinette, and then towards Brera there's Hidden Forest Market that has its own particular style and is definitely worth a visit. Then I generally make my way towards the Cinque Vie, to two shops that are Wait and See and Funky Table. There, lunch is usually at Zibo or Cuochi Iteneranti, but my favourite lunch in Milan would definitely be the street food in Via Paolo Sarpi, particularly Ravioleria Sarpi and Beijing Traditional Roll. I'll go towards the Navigli around late afternoon. It's the best time to go, especially for an aperitivo at Iter. They do fantastic cocktails and on Sundays they do a 'pranzo della nonna', a grandma's lunch. Each week the region changes, so one week you'll have a typical lunch from a Lombard nonna, that of your nonna from Piedmont, and so on. And it's right here at your favourite bar.'

Giorgia Dell'Orto, Ambroeus, Isola

Rachael Martin

all new arrivals: @ambroeus.milano.
All pieces can be bought online and
delivered.

Ambroeus, Via Pastrengo, 15, 02 3659 2537,
Tues–Sun 10.30 am – 7.30 pm.
www.ambroeusmilano.it

Delphine Vintage (vintage women's clothing and accessories)

Vintage clothing, accessories and bijoux
from the early twentieth century up
until the 1970s, especially items from the
1930s, 1940s and 1950s. The overall look
is feminine and romantic, and includes
beautiful dresses such as 1920s fringed
flapper dresses and beaded dresses and
1960s and 1970s prints. They also have
lace bodices, costume jewellery and a
variety of other accessories such as lace
pieces, buttons, veils, hats and fabric
flowers.

Delphine Vintage, Via Guiglielmo Pepe, 16, 347
734 7030, Mon–Sat 10 am – 8 pm.
www.delphinevintage.com

Le Vintage (women's clothing and accessories)

Le Vintage is a women's clothing
boutique that, in spite of what its name
may suggest, sells mainly new items,
but with a definite air of vintage luxury
and retro style. Owner Silvia Bertolaja
was inspired by the boutiques that were
once along Carnaby Street, and chooses
distinct pieces that often include one-off
pieces from the world of fashion and art.

Le Vintage. Le Vintage

The shop also stocks Le Solferine shoes
designed by Silvia and artisan made, the
same shoes that are at Le Solferine on
Via Solferino (See page 86).

Le Vintage, via Garigliano, 4, 02 6931 1885,
Mon–Fri 10 am – 8 pm, Sat 11 am – 2 pm,
3 – 7 pm. Facebook @levintage.eu

Live in Vintage

Live in Vintage sells women's vintage
designer clothing, accessories and
bijoux from the 1920s through to the
1990s. They specialise in tailored

clothing and particularly look for good quality materials and also specialise in clothes from the 1970s and 1980s.

Live in Vintage, Via Genova Thaon di Revel, 328 5372421 / 347 6039319, Tues–Fri 10.30 am – 1.30 pm, 4 – 7.30 pm, Sat 10.30 am – 1.30 pm, 3.30 – 7 pm. **www.liveinvintagemilano.com**

Monica Castiglioni (jewellery)

Monica Castiglioni, daughter of designer Achille Castiglioni, is both an acclaimed jeweller and photographer, and lives between her ateliers in Milan's Isola district, Brooklyn and Ortigia on the beautiful island of Syracuse, in Sicily. Her jewellery has very much a sculptural quality, and indeed she also makes sculptures. Her work has an organic feel, unusual shapes, often in bronze but also in silver, Pyrex, felt and 3D nylon. Pieces are mostly forged using the lost-wax technique, an ancient casting technique that uses wax as the mould into which metal is poured. Castiglioni is inspired by flower pistils that recurrently appear in her work, symbols of order and balance within apparent chaos. If you're interested in jewellery design, her shop is a definite must-visit. Her work is also for sale in the bookshops of various museums such as the Metropolitan Museum of Art in New York, the Cooper Hewitt in New York, and the MoMA in San Francisco.

Monica Castiglioni, Via Pastrengo, 4, 02 8723 7979, Thurs–Sat 11 am – 8 pm. Also Wednesday by appointment; ring 02 8723 7979 or write to milano@monicacastiglioni.com.) **www.monicacastiglioni.com**

Rapa (womenswear, childrenswear)

Sara Rotta Loria spent ten years designing childrenswear and then also started designing womenswear when she opened her shop Rapa. She produces two collections a year. The style is easy chic Made in Italy, and the emphasis is on comfort and originality with softly shaped dresses and wide-legged trousers. The shop also hosts collections by other artisans producing jewellery, shoes and scarves that change on a periodical basis.

Rapa, via Pastrengo, 5A, 02 2316 7868, Tues–Fri 10.30 am – 2.30 pm, 3.30–7.30 pm, Sat 11 am – 7 pm. www.rapamilano.com

8

VIA PAOLO SARPI
Home of Milan's Chinatown

M2 Garibaldi, M5 Garibaldi, M2 Moscova

Via Paolo Sarpi is the heart of Milan's Chinatown and historically has strong links with Milan's textiles industry. It has benefitted from recent urban regeneration and is now a pedestrian street, offering restaurants, cafés, bars, clothing and speciailist food shops. Via Paolo Sarpi is also host to Oriental Design Week, the Oriental fuorisalone of Milan Design Week. (**www.orientaldesignweek.org**)

COFFEE

While you're here, visit **Pasticceria Martesana** for exquisite pasticcini, especially their bigné with Chantilly cream.

Pasticceria Martesana, Via Paolo Sarpi, 62, 02 9926 5069, Mon–Sat 7.30 am – 8 pm, Sun 8 am – 7.30 pm.
www.martesanamilano.com

LUNCH

Ravioleria Sarpi

Go for award-winning takeaway ravioli at great prices.

Ravioleria Sarpi, via Paolo Sarpi, 25/27, 331 887, 10 am – 3 pm, 4 – 10 pm every day.
Facebook @ravioleriasarpi

SHOPPING

Cappelleria Melegari (milliner's)

Cappelleria Melegari have been making and selling hats since 1914 alongside a wide range of some of the best names in hats internationally, including Borsalino. This is one of those shops of once upon a time, where you walk through various rooms literally filled with hats, and where the assistants will advise you on the very best shape and fit. Go up to the second floor where they have their own workshop.

Cappelleria Melegari, Via Paolo Sarpi, 19, 02 312094, Mon 3.30 – 7.30 pm, Tues–Sat 9.30 am – 1 pm, 3.30 – 7.30 pm.
www.cappelleriamelegarimilano.com

May Faber. May Faber

May Faber

May Faber (men's tailoring)

When May Faber opened in 2013, the aim was to create a tailor's that draws on tailoring traditions in terms of quality of materials and craftsmanship, but give it a modern twist to fit in with the style desired by young men today. Here you'll find a world of suits and shirts in various styles and colours. Whether it's a suit, shirt or waistcoat, every detail is chosen by the clients from a vast selection of fabrics offered, all is made in Italy, including fabrics that are often outside the usual suit and shirt fabrics. Italian rapper J-Ax is one of the celebrities they dress, alongside the local businessmen. The shop also offers a monthly barber's service, for that extra special touch for clients.

May Faber, Via Giuseppe Prina, 1, 324 887 3665, Tues–Fri 10 am – 2 pm, 3.30–7.30 pm, Sat 10 am – 1 pm, 2 – 7 pm. **www.mayfaber.com**

MENSWEAR AND TAILORING

Italy has a strong history of tailoring, and is a world leader on an international level. Neopolitan tailor Gennaro Rubinacci opened his tailor's in Naples in 1932 and developed the Neopolitan jacket, lighter and without the usual padding and much more suitable for a southern climate. In Milan it was generally all about the precision of the cut with stiffer jackets and more constructed shoulders, and preferably set off with a crisp white shirt. Later, Giorgio Armani revolutionised the suit, both for men and for women, and gave women a new working wardrobe.

Adobe Stock

THE FASHION LOVER'S LIST: MILAN MARKETS

Don't forget the markets. Each area in Milan has its 'mercato rionale', or neighbourhood market, and you'd be amazed what you can pick up: labels, shoes, cashmere, leather, it's generally all here as well as food stalls. Here are a few to keep on your list.

1. **Via Fauché** (Corso Sempione) It's a favourite with the locals with its stalls of discounted designer and vintage clothing and accessories. You'll need to look, but there are designer bargains to be had. Tuesday 8 am – 2 pm and Saturday 8 am – 6 pm.

2. **Via San Marco (Brera)** Go for MaxMara, Marella, Sport Max and many other designer brands, cashmere, shoes, second-hand and new designer bags and other leather bags. Fashion stalls are mixed in with the food stalls, and if you're looking for a place to pose nonchalantly beside the funghi porcini in an Instagram–ready tableau of Milanese life, this is your place. Mondays and Thursdays, 7.30 am – 2 pm.

3. **Viale Papiniano** (starts near Tortona) This is your typical everyday local market, and quite a big one at that. It stretches along the middle of Viale Papianino and there's plenty to see. There's also plenty that might not really catch your eye, but keep looking as there are bargains to be found including stock designer goods and leather bags. Go to nearby Pasticceria Martesana (Via Cagliero, 14) if you find yourself needing a break. They do the most amazing pasticcini, just in case you were wondering. Tuesdays 8 am – 2 pm, Saturdays 8 am – 5 pm.

PORTA GENOVA/PORTA TICINESE/NAVIGLI
Vintage, streetware and quirky boutiques

M2 Porta Genova; trams 2 and 14 go all the way down from Piazza del Duomo along Via Torino, Via Cesare Correnti and then onto Corso Genova. Tram number 3 from the centre goes down Corso di Porta Ticinese.

Corso Genova marks the beginning of the Ticinese district of Milan that stretches down to Porta Genova, Milan's oldest railway station, and the Navigli, Milan's canal system, which was begun during the twelfth century. It also includes the southern part of Corso di Porta Ticinese, the street leading on from Via Torino that comes down from the Piazza del Duomo. Porta means

Porta Ticinese. Rachael Martin

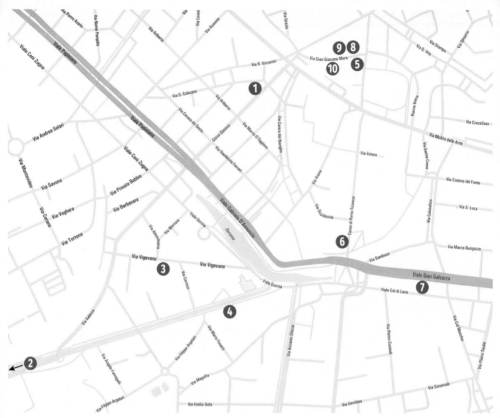

PORTA GENOVA / PORTA TICINESE / NAVIGLI. 1 Biffi Boutique, 2 MV% Ceramics Design, 3 Salvatore & Marie, 4 Pourquoi Moi, 5 Frip, 6 Serendeepity, 7 Wok Store, 8 Bivio, 9 Cavalli e Nastri, 10 Groupies Vintage

gate, and these were both two gates in the south of Milan. For the Milanese, Porta Ticinese is also known as Porta Cicca. The writings on the walls here read like a metropolitan poem, with political messages, songs, poetry and philosophy. It comes with its own subtitle, a sign attached to the wall above the sign on the dark pink building with the wrought iron balcony and the ivy trailing down: 'The street of irony. It's not a consequence but a necessity.' There's also the history, the calm atmosphere of Piazza di Sant'Eustorgio with its beautiful church of the same name that has its origins in the third–fourth centuries, and the Columns of San Lorenzo and the Basilica of San Lorenzo, which Leonardo da Vinci thought was Milan's most beautiful church. They date back to the fourth and fifth centuries and Milan's days as Mediolanum, capital of the Roman Empire. And it's all mixed up with the mix of Milanese streetwear, vintage shops, records, some of the city's coolest boutiques and tattoo parlours that make up Porta Ticinese.

Shopping-wise, the Navigli, as Milan's canal area is known, is also synonymous with vintage shops, quirky boutiques and a plethora of bars for that much-needed coffee or relaxed aperitivo. It's one of Milan's most romantic, almost poetic, landscapes with views along the canals, glimpses of an older Milano, and a far more alternative feel, and if you've never seen a sunset over the Navigli Grande, you really should. While you're sitting in one of the bars sipping your expertly mixed cocktail, you'd be forgiven for thinking that these are the types of places that have been around for years. Actually they haven't. The Navigli's nightlife and shopping scene belongs to recent times, whereas the history of the Navigli dates back to the twelfth century, when they were used to transport marble from Cadoglia to build the Duomo. They also supported Milan's textile industry that dates back as far as the medieval period and transported other goods and supplies. Nowadays there are two main canals that remain, the Naviglio Grande and the Naviglio Pavese, along with the Darsena that functioned as the port and was given a facelift at the beginning of the century. The others were all covered over in the late 1920s.

To see the Navigli as they were during the last century, there's a series of fashion photographs taken by Italian photographer Ugo Mulas for Jole Veneziani that were published in the magazine *Settimo Giorno,* on the 27 November 1958. In one of them there is a woman standing in a gold evening dress and long white gloves, a sparkling hairband in her bouffant hair, a woman that belongs to the world of Alta Moda and evenings at Teatro alla Scala. Behind her are the loading hoppers and crane of a working canal, signs of a post-war world that was rebuilding itself after a second world war.* It's a stark contrast of two worlds. The Navigli were home to a community of shopkeepers, artisans and people who worked in the surrounding industries. Signs of this artisan past are still present in the brass signs outside the big wooden gates that lead into the courtyards, and along the Vicolo dei Lavandai, the communal washing area where women would wash clothes for the Milanese public up until the 1950s. Nowadays the alley is home to art galleries and boutiques. Number 47, Ripa di Porta Ticinese is where much-loved Milanese poet Alda Merini, known affectionately as 'Poet of the Navigli' lived. Look for the stone bridge that was named after her on the tenth anniversary of her death in 2019. Personal belongings and objects can be found at the Casa delle Arti – Spazio Alda Merini (Via Magolfa, 32) in a reconstruction of her bedroom on the first floor. The wall outside has the installation 'Wall of Dolls', a stark and painful reminder of the number of femicides that take place every year.

*Frisa, Mattirolo, Tronchi, Bellissima: L'Italia Dell'Alta Moda: 1945-1968, pp.257-258

THE APERITIVO, MADE IN MILAN

When in Milan, go for an aperitivo. The Milanese claim the ritual of the aperitivo as their own, and one that goes back to the days when Ernest Hemingway drank at Biffi in Galleria Vittorio Emanuele II alongside others from the world of the arts, music, film and society. Try an Aperol, Milan's native aperitivo, a Campari spritz (Prosecco and Campari bitter) or a Negroni (red Vermouth, Campari and gin). At one time the aperitivo involved traditional accompaniments of mainly peanuts, olives or crisps, and a buffet that generally outruled dinner. Nowadays the choice includes sourced finger-food from slow food producers that produce high quality local foods, often with respect to culinary tradition. Where to drink? The Navigli and Porta Venezia are all good places to head for aperitivo, while Galleria Vittorio Emanuele II offers a classic Milanese experience that's not to be missed. The area around the nineteenth-century Arco della Pace offers plenty of bars and cafés with tables along the street and the popular Bhangrabar.

Bar Basso is the legendary bar that's home to the Negroni Sbagliato. 'Sbagliato' means wrong – barman Mirko Stocchetto added sparkling wine instead of gin. Ceresio 7 is owned by twins Dean and Dan Caten of DSquared2 in what was originally a 1930s Enel electricity company building. The retro rooftop restaurant has a pool and great views of the Porta Nuova skyscrapers. Just Cavalli is Roberto Cavalli's restaurant and nightclub with an interior as glamorous as you would expect. In the historic Torre Branca, designed by Gio Ponti in the 1930s, it offers views all over Milan. It's popular with celebrities, and if you want to get in you need to dress up.

Bhangrabar, Corso Sempione, 1, 02 3493 4469, Mon–Sun 6 pm – 2 am. **www.bhangrabar.it**

Bar Basso, Via Plinio, 39, 02 2940 0580, 9 am – 1.15 am (closed on Tuesdays). **www.barbasso.com**

Ceresio 7, Via Ceresio, 7, 02 3103 9221, Mon–Sun bar 12.30 pm – 1 am, restaurant 12.30 – 3 pm, 12.30 pm – 1 am. **www.ceresio7.com**

Just Cavalli, Torre Branca, Via Luigi Camoens, 02 311817, Mon–Sun 7.30 pm – 5.30 am. **www.justcavallimilano.com**

EAT AND DRINK

Around the Navigli, it's all about the aperitivo. Here's a selection.

Iter

The sign reads 'From Italy to the world', the concept is a voyage that begins with breakfast and ends with late-night cocktails, a base of quality Italian products and a menu that will take you to a different place every six months. The atmosphere is relaxed, and you can sit and eat at the bar. 'Domenica dalla nonna' is their 'Sunday lunch at grandma's' that takes you all around Italy and the world.

Via Mario Fusetti, 1, 02 3599 9589, Mon–Fri 7.30 am – 2 am, Sat–Sun 9 am – 2 am. Instagram @iter_milano, Facebook @ IterFromItalyToTheWorld

Mag Café

Speakeasy-style bar, complete with easy armchairs, low tables and various curios, and where cocktails are an art form.

Ripa di Porta Ticinese, 43, 02 3956 2875, Mon–Sun 7.30 am – 1.30 am. Instagram @magcafe, Facebook @magcafemilano

Rita

Another favourite for cocktails, both classic and revisited. Home to the gin zen: freshly-crushed ginger, gin, lime, soda, and crushed ice.

Via Angelo Fumagalli, 1, 02 837 2865, Mon 6.30 pm – 2 am, Sun 12.30 – 4 pm, 6.30 pm – 2 am. Instagram @ritacocktails, Facebook @RitaCocktails

SHOPPING

Corso Genova/Navigli

One word of advice: things start much later along the Navigli, so if you're planning

Navigli. Rachael Martin

on visiting the area, it's best to come along mid-afternoon and stay for an aperitivo. Nowadays Tortona provides the competition as far as contemporary cool is concerned, yet the Navigli movida still holds strong, and is best sampled outside at the tables along the Naviglio Grande on a balmy night. I've included a few suggestions below. Feel free to just wander though and enjoy at leisure.

Biffi Boutiques (womenswear, menswear)

Biffi Boutiques Milano is the original boutique that sisters Rosy and Adele Biffi opened in the mid-1960s. Rosy Biffi had been to London, come back and

started selling clothes by designers such as Biba, Quorum, which was the boutique founded by designer Alice Pollock and included designers such as Ossie Clark and Celia Birtwell, and Mary Quant – all names that were revolutionary at the time. The boutique, restyled by Milanese architect Gae Aulenti, has continued to lead the way over the years in the search for Italian and international cutting-edge fashion. Go there for designer names that include Alexander McQueen, Bottega Veneta, Comme des Garçons, Dior Homme, Givenchy, Gucci, Fendi, Facetasm, Loewe, Junya Watanabe, Marni, Plan C, Sacai, Stella McCartney and Italian designers Alanui's colourful knitwear inspired by native American

Biffi Boutique. Biffi Boutiques

Biffi Boutique. Biffi Boutiques

patterns and colours. They also have MSGM, Jacquemus, Tiziano Guardini's sustainable creations, Roger Vivier shoes and accessories, jewellery by Bea Bongiasca, Golden Goose Deluxe Brand and Stella Jean's designs. Biffi Boutiques Group also owns Biffi B-Contemporary sportswear and casualwear boutique that sells labels such as Ami, Adidas Originals, BD Baggies, Department 5, Paul Smith and Stone Island.

Biffi Boutiques, Corso Genova, 6, 02 8311 6052, Mon 3 – 7.30 pm, Tues–Sat 10 am – 7.30 pm. Biffi B-Contemporary, Corso Genova, 5, 02 8311 6044, Mon 3 – 7.30 pm, Tues – Fri 10 am – 1 pm, 3 – 7.30 pm, Sat 10 am – 7.30 pm. **www.biffi.com**

MV% Ceramics Design. Mariavera Chiari

MV% Ceramics Design (ceramics)

Mariavera Chiari makes and sells ceramics in her workshop along the Naviglio Grande. After studying architecture at the Politecnico of Milan, she worked for several years with Cino Zucchi architects. She then opened her studio in 2002 where she produces items for the home and garden, all under her name MV% Ceramics Design. Her brother joined her in 2008. From espresso cups with spoons that are available in twenty-four different colours, to vegetable wall decorations, plates and ceramic letters, each piece is hand cut and glazed, and therefore unique. Mariavera finds her inspiration in nature: clouds, raindrops, stars, flowers and animals. Since 2002 she's taken part in the Salon Maison & Objet in Paris. It's a great place

to go if you're looking for gift ideas and that special little something to pack in your suitcase.

MV% Ceramics Design, Alzaia Naviglio Grande, 156, 349 067 9815, 349 067 9815, Mon–Fri 9 am – 1.30 pm, Sat 11 am – 7 pm. www.mv-ceramicsdesign.it

Salvatore & Marie (fashion and design)

If you're looking for something slightly unusual and original, Salvatore and Marie offer an eclectic mix of design and fashion in their shop along Via Vigevano. They sell their own unique pieces, which they design and produce in collaboration with other artists. Pieces are designed by Salvatore and Marie and are either made locally or made manually by Salvatore and Marie themselves. There is also a small selection of sourced pieces that are designed and made all over Italy and the world. You might not be able to take home a bookcase or a mirror, but they have smaller objects such as jewellery, fruit bowls and cups that may definitely catch your eye.

Salvatore & Marie, Via Vigevano, 33, 02 8942 2152, Mon 3.30–7.30 pm, Tues–Sat 10.30 am – 1 pm, 3.30 – 7.30 pm. Instagram @salvatoremarieshop

Pourquoi Moi (women's vintage clothing and accessories)

For vintage clothing, head straight to Porquoi Moi along the Naviglio Grande. Juliana Osei, originally from London, has been selling vintage clothing, shoes, accessories and bijoux for years and

Pourquoi Moi. Rachael Martin

Pourquoi Moi. Rachael Martin

along the Naviglio Grande, together with her partner Keith Livingstone, since May 2008. The shop specialises in international fashion brands, Scandinavian pieces and Made in Italy, simply because the quality of Made in Italy is so good. Juliana loves Finnish cottons such as Marimekko and Vuokko, which offer simple shapes with often complex patterns as they tend to be extremely good quality and wash well again and again. She also favours brands such as Ungaro, Krizia, Jean Charles De Castelbajac, Roberta di Camerino, Louis Feraud and Guy Laroche. Also look out for top level vintage boutique fashion such as Valditevere dresses, Emilio Pucci, Mario Pucci Cecconi blouses, Pancaldi silk and wool skirts and blouses, Pirovano and Lancetti clothing and leather goods, Emilia Bellini clothing, (Cadette where Moschino worked at the beginning of his career), Livio Di Simone's (Capri) hand-printed, brightly coloured prints, Gattinoni coats and dresses and De Parisini prints and silk jersey dresses. These are all good quality, sartorial Made in Italy pieces with excellent fabrics and craftsmanship.

Pourquoi Moi, Ripa di Porta Ticinese, 33, 339 579 2838, by appointment.
Instagram @pourquoimoivintage

Juliana Osei. Rachael Martin

SELLING VINTAGE ALONG THE NAVIGLI – JULIANA OSEI

'Historically, let's say from the 1980s, the Navigli has always been known as an area for vintage and artisan shops. It's very picturesque here as the canal environment creates a nice atmosphere, especially in spring and summer. For me the most important thing was that if you're looking to open a shop you'll be going there for most of your day, most of the week, for many years of your life. So, at that point you should try at least to choose somewhere attractive that's a pleasure to go to every day. That's why I headed straight to the Naviglio Grande and I found the shop that very same day! In that sense I feel lucky. I could think of worse areas to work!'

Juliana Osei, Pourquoi Moi

ALSO VISIT...

Set in an old fifteenth-century courtyard along Naviglio Grande, **Anthropology** sells clothes for both men and women that are a mix of Made in Italy and international labels. If you're looking for a leather jacket, **Guendj** has models

from the 1970s, 1980s and 1990s. Head to streetwear store **Special** for sneakers.

Finally, don't forget the market along Viale Papiniano, which takes place on Tuesdays (8 am – 2 pm) and Saturdays (8 am – 5 pm).

Anthropology, Alzaia Naviglio Grande, 4, 02 3663 9276, Mon–Sun 11 am – 7 pm. **www.anthropologymilano.com**

Guendj, Ripa di Porta Ticinese, 47, 339 7242495, 347 996 8043, Tues 10 am – 1 pm, 4 – 8 pm, Wed–Thurs 10 am – 1 pm, 3.30 – 7.30 pm, Fri 10 am – 1 pm, 4.30 – 11.30 pm, Sat 10.30 am – 1 pm, 3.30 – 11.30 pm, Sun 10 am – 7 pm (apart from last Sunday of month when there's the Mercatone dell'Antiquariato 10 am – 8 pm). **www.guendj.com**

Special, Corso di Porta Ticinese, 80, 02 8905 6307, Mon 3.30 – 7.30 pm, Tues–Sat 10.30 am – 1.30 pm, 2.30 – 7.30 pm, Sun 2 – 7 pm. **www.specialmilano.com**

Rachael Martin

PORTA TICINESE

Frip (concept store)

Frip specialises in British, French and Scandinavian brands, including Acme Studios, Marios, Hope, Aries, Cmmn Swdn, Drôle de Monsieur and ATP. They sell both menswear and womenswear alongside independent magazines, accessories, shoes and bags. Their philosophy is based upon offering contemporary unique items that also stand the test of time. The shop is run by a husband and wife team – she's the stylist and he's the DJ – that has been keeping it all fresh for over twenty years.

Frip, Corso di Porta Ticinese, 16, 02 832 1360, Mon 3.30 – 7.30 pm, Tues–Sat 11 am – 2 pm, 3–8 pm, Sun 3.30 – 7 pm. **www.frip.it**

Serendeepity (music, magazines, books, vintage clothing and accessories)

Walk in and there's vinyl, alongside street art, graphic novels, independent magazines and fairly niche music-related books. You need to go downstairs for their selection of vintage clothing and accessories.

Serendeepity, Corso di Porta Ticinese, 100, 02 8940 0420, Mon 3 – 8 pm, Tues–Sat 10.30 am – 8 pm, Sun 3-8 pm. **www.serendeepity.it**

Wok Store (concept store)

Inspired by London and New York, this dynamic and continuously evolving concept store was opened in 2007. The shop offers an energetic mix of fashion, design and events. It not only has some of the most interesting names in contemporary fashion, but hosts art and fashion exhibitions, DJ sets and fashion shows by emerging designers. Collections change and include limited editions, capsule collections, various collaborations, and an attention to organic or recycled materials.

Wok Store, Viale Col di Lana, 5a, 02 3656 8742, Mon 3 – 7.30 pm, Tues 10.30 am – 2 pm, 3 – 7.30 pm, Wed–Sat 10.30 am – 7.30 pm. Instagram @wokstore

VIA GIAN GIACOMO MORA

Via Gian Giacomo Mora links Corso di Porta Ticinese to Corso Genova, and has several vintage and second-hand clothing shops.

Bivio (second-hand and vintage clothing and accessories)

Bivio is the clothing exchange to go look for second-hand and vintage pieces such as Jimmy Choo, Prada, Chanel, Alexander Wang and Bottega Veneta, as well as high street favourites such as Zara. Clothes, shoes, hats, sunglasses, bags: the choice is yours. They sell both men's and women's clothing and it's definitely worth taking a look if you're in the area. They've also had Yves Saint Laurent evening dresses.

Bivio: womenswear, Via Gian Giacomo Mora, 4; menswear, via Giangiacomo Mora, 14; womenswear and menswear, via Lambro, 12 (Porta Venezia); 02 5810 8691, all shops open Mon–Sun 11 am – 7.30 pm. **www.biviomilano.it**

Cavalli e Nastri (vintage clothing and accessories)

These are the other two shops belonging to the same people who have Cavalli e Nastri along Via Brera.

They have items from the early 1800s right up to the 1970s, and also stock contemporary pieces by designers such as Gucci, Chanel and Comme des Garçons. One of their most significant pieces was a mid-nineteenth-century dress by Charles Frederick Worth, the Lincolnshire-born textile merchant apprentice who went to Paris, became one of the most famous designers of the time, and enjoyed the patronage of Empress Eugénie, wife of Napoleon III. His dresses became extremely popular

Cavalli e Nastri. Cavalli e Nastri

Cavalli e Nastri. Cavalli e Nastri

among the aristocracy and the wealthy in both Europe and the USA, and the particular dress in question became part of a costume exhibition in Mendrisio. They also have a large collection of Biki in their archives. Come here for Italian, French and other vintage clothing, and leather goods from the 1920s onwards. They also provide a service whereby pieces can be made up according to models that clients select. There are two shops along the street. Womenswear and accessories is at number 12,

while number 3 stocks menswear and accessories.

Cavalli e Nastri, Via Gian Giacomo Mora, 12, 02 8940 9453, Mon–Sat 10.30 am – 7.30 pm, Sun 12 – 7.30 pm. **www.cavallienastri.com**

Groupies Vintage (women's and men's vintage clothing and accessories)

Alice Cipriani's vintage shop takes its inspiration from the subcultures of 1970s and 1980s London. The idea of the shop is to try to recreate the atmosphere of

the groupies of these years and of the social, cultural and sexual revolution that took place. The shop works on buy, sell and trade, and you can find selected vintage from the 1950s to the 1980s, a lot of which is from London and Berlin. There's also recycled vintage – that is, clothes that have been given new life through a contemporary lens.

Groupies Vintage, Via Gian Giacomo Mora, 7, 02 8942 3882, Mon 2.30 – 7.30 pm, Tues–Sat 11 am – 7.30 pm.
www.groupiesvintage.com

Mercatone dell'Antiquariato

The monthly Mercatone dell'Antiquariato really draws in the crowds along the Naviglio Grande. It stretches from Viale Gorizia to the bridge of Via Valenza, and spreads into the surrounding streets. The market began in 1982. It's Milan's biggest antiques market and stretches for nearly 2 km along the canal and has around 350 market stalls. Carefully selected sellers offer everything from vintage clothing to antiques and mid-century furniture, homeware and other goods. If you're wanting to pick up an Yves Saint Laurent trenchcoat or a vintage Gucci handbag, this might be your lucky day. Over recent years the vintage selection has grown as interest in vintage clothing has grown. Via Corsico and Via Paoli are particularly good for quality vintage. The market takes place on the last Sunday of every month between 9 am and 7 pm, apart from December when it is brought forward, according to how Christmas falls. Check their online calendar for dates.

WHY YOU REALLY SHOULD TO GO TO MILAN AT CHRISTMAS AT LEAST ONCE IN YOUR LIFE

Treat yourself to Christmas, Milanese style. Apart from offering some of the best in shopping, this is when Milan is at its most magical with lights, huge Christmas trees in both the Galleria Vittorio Emanuele II and in Piazza Duomo and others around the city, and stunning shop window displays. For the latter, you have to visit Rinascente, whose Christmas displays are always spectacular. Don't forget a wander around the Golden Quad. During the week it can be surprisingly quiet, leaving you the space and tranquillity to just soak it all up.

Christmas in Milan traditionally begins on the feast of the city's patron saint, Sant'Ambrogio (Saint Ambrose) on 7 December. It's also opening night of the opera season at La Scala opera house and

time of the Fiera degli Oh Bej Oh Bej market, which dates back to medieval times and takes place near the Castello Sforzesco. If you're planning a pre-Christmas shopping trip, this is a great weekend to come. Throughout the Christmas period, Christmas markets are packed with delicious food and artisan products. Milan is home to the Christmas panettone, as well as many other goodies that you might want to put in your suitcase. Go skating down at the Darsena Christmas village near the Navigli, and if you've never seen the Navigli dressed for Christmas, it really is one of Milan's prettiest sights.

Finally, don't miss Piazza del Duomo by night. Visit the Museo del Novecento and go up to the Lucio Fontana room where the view of Fontana's *Neon Structure* with the Duomo, Galleria Vittorio Emanuele II and the huge Christmas tree in the Piazza del Duomo is truly spectacular. It brings together different periods of Milanese history, all through the lens of Christmas in Milan.

Galleria Vittorio Emanuele II. © Comune di Milano

Navigli. © Comune di Milano

ZONA TORTONA:
Vintage, streetware and quirky boutiques

M2 Porta Genova

On the other side of the Porta Genova railway track is Via Tortona in what was once an area of factories, warehouses, workshops and the housing built for the people who worked there, characterised by the shared communal balconies running along each floor known as 'casa di ringhiera'. The arrival of the railway station in 1875 was significant. The area was designated as Milan's first industrial centre by the businessmen and manufacturers involved. The railway station allowed access to the factories, and the transformation of what was previously agricultural land into a thriving industrial heartland. It was also where the coal arrived to heat the homes of the city's residents.

Today Via Tortona and the adjoining streets, or Zona Tortona as it's known, has established itself at the forefront of the Milanese design scene and achieved worldwide fame through Milan's Design Week, whose principal event is the Salone Internazionale del Mobile, Milan's Furniture Fair. Such a transformation began towards the end of the 1980s when the various industries began to move outside the city, with the opening of Superstudio 13, the photography studio that was opened by Gisella Borioli and Flavio Lucchini in 1983, which is now also a venue for fashion shows and other events. The area is also home to fashion-world headquarters such as Armani, Diesel, Ermengildo Zegna and Moncler, alongside boutiques, workshops, temporary pop-up shops with trendy restaurants, bars and traditional osterias. The annual Design Week in April is when Tortona really

TORTONA. 1 Armani/Silos, 2 Fondazione Gianfranco Ferré, 3 Bottegatre, 4 Carmen Veca, 5 Memèm, 6 Nonostante Marras

comes to life. Events take place all over Milan as part of the city's Fuorisalone (literally, outside the showroom) programme but it's Zona Tortona that's one of the hotspots. Wander around buildings filled with the latest design objects for your house to drool over, hear the DJs, eat, drink, and generally make the most of one of the best weeks of the year. Whereas Fashion Weeks are generally the realm of exclusive invitations, Design Week is an event that everyone can enjoy.

Just a few blocks away is the swimming pool, Milansport Piscina Solari, in the park of the same name that was built above the city's slaughterhouse. Missoni staged their first Milan show at the swimming pool in November 1967. Models sat on inflatable furniture designed by Quasar Khanh, with a grand finale when they all jumped into the pool. The fashion world took note. Fashion journalist

Maria Pezzi said that it captured the fashion of the time in Italian newspaper *Il Giorno* and Missoni started its way to becoming one of the biggest names in Italian fashion.

Don't forget the walkway dedicated to Biki (see page 61). If you come by metro you'll walk through it on your way to Zona Tortona.

EAT AND DRINK

BRUNCH

God Save the Food

Brunches and sandwich platters, along with wok dishes, eggs and salads.

God Save the Food, Via Tortona, 34, 02 8942 3806, Mon–Fri 7.30 am – 12 am, Sat/Sun 8 am – 12 am. **www.godsavethefood.it**

DINNER

Osteria del Binari

Go for Milanese favourites and freshly-made pasta.

Osteria del Binari, Via Tortona, 1, 02 8940 6753, open Mon–Sun 12.30 pm – 2.30 pm, 7.30 pm – 11 pm. **www.osteriadelbinari.com**

APERITIVO

The Botanical Club

Go for cocktails and an international menu.

The Botanical Club, Via Tortona, 33, restaurant: Mon–Sun lunch 12.30 – 3pm, dinner 6.30 pm – 10.30 pm (closed Sunday evening); bar open Mon–Sat until 1 am. **www.thebotanicalclub.com**

Al Fresco

Popular for aperitivo, and again, especially during Fashion Week. It has a romantic air to it with huge windows that face onto the garden, and when it's all lit up in the evening the atmosphere really is quite magical.

Al Fresco, Via Savona, 50, 02 4953 3630, Mon–Sat 12.30 – 2.30 pm, 7.30 – 10.30 pm. **www. alfrescomilano.it**

CULTURE STOP

BASE

Multi-functional cultural centre set in what was once the Ansaldo factory. See their website for details of various events.

Base, Via Bergognone, 34, **www.base.milano.it**

MUDEC

Home to intercultural exhibitions of international standing, and worth keeping on your radar to see what's on.

Mudec, Via della Tortona, 56, 02 54917, Mon 2.30 – 7.30 pm, Tues/Wed/Fri/Sun 9.30 am – 7.30 pm, Thurs/Sat 9.30 am – 10.30 pm. **www.mudec.it**

Teatro alla Scala Ansaldo workshops

The workshops are now open to the public, so book a guided tour to enter the fascinating world of costume and stage design in what was once the industrial settlement of the Ansaldo steel company. The workshops are housed in three pavilions, dedicated to director Luchino

Visconti, set designer Nicola Benois and costume designer Luigi Sapelli, also known as Caramba. This is where stage sets are crafted and costumes made to appear on one of the most famous stages in the world. To book a tour, email servizi@civita.it

Laboratori Scala Ansaldo, Via Bergagnone, 34, 02 335 3521. **www.teatroallascala.org**

White Milano

White Milano is Milan's street fashion and culture event that takes place in Zona Tortona. See **www.whitestreetmarket.it** for details.

ARMANI/SILOS

The Armani/Silos is situated in what was once the granary of a large multinational company, hence the name Armani/Silos. It was opened in 2015 to celebrate forty years of the designer's career, the year that also saw the Milan Expo and Giorgio Armani as the Special Ambassador for fashion. The

Armani/Silos entrance. Davide Lovatti

exhibition space has a rotating permanent collection of the designer's works that are displayed according to theme and give a comprehensive viewpoint of the length and breadth of the designer's career. The top floor holds an extensive digital archive that consists of sketches, technical drawings and other materials from ready-to-wear collections, including fashion show photos, videos and advertising campaigns. Temporary design and photography exhibitions are also held.

Armani/Silos, Via Bergognone, 40, 02 9163 0010, Wed-Sun 11 am – 7 pm **www.armani.com**

GIORGIO ARMANI

Giorgio Armani was born in 1934, in Piacenza, a town in the north of Emilia Romagna. He went to Milan originally to study medicine at the University of Milan, and while he was studying went off to join the army for the compulsory military service. When he came out of the army in 1957, he never went back to medicine. He found a job as a window

dresser in La Rinascente instead, and later became a salesman in the men's department. Armani stayed there for seven years, after which he went into fashion design, starting at Nino Cerruti for their new men's clothing line, Hitman.

In 1975 he set up his own business with Sergio Galeotti and produced his first men's clothing range. The same year he showed his first womenswear collection. Diane Keaton wore Armani when she received her Oscar in 1978, but it was when Richard Gere wore a total of thirty Armani suits in the 1980 film *American Gigolo* that a lifelong relationship with Hollywood began that would include films such as *The Untouchables* in 1987, Martin Scorsese's *Goodfellas* and *The Wolf of Wall Street*, and American TV series *Miami Vice*. Armani's androgynous approach softened male fashion and gave women's fashion a stronger edge and a new way of dressing in an elegant, essential, understated key. Not only did it become associated with the Made in Italy look, but in this sense, it is also very Milanese. Whether it's clothing, eyewear, interior design or jewels, Giorgio Armani represents above all a distinctive lifestyle choice. In 2005 he showed his first haute couture collection, known as Armani Privé, in Paris.

FONDAZIONE GIANFRANCO FERRÉ

The Fondazione Gianfranco Ferré was created in February 2008 to bring together the documents and materials that chart the designer's professional career, and to make these available to the public while promoting and undertaking projects that adhere to the Gianfranco Ferré philosophy and culture of design. The foundation consists of an archive/museum of over 90,000 sketches, drawings, photographs, films and video footage, magazines, press reviews, press releases and personal writings by the designer himself and a digital database of collections season by season, all digitally stored. The foundation also takes care of the archive of around 3,000 pieces of clothing and accessories from the womenswear, menswear and haute couture collections. Initiatives are organised both in Italy and internationally and include lectures, conferences, exhibitions and other events that relate to the work of Ferré and to the world of contemporary fashion and aesthetics in general. The foundation has solid links with Milan-based fashion universities and institutions, and the objective of becoming a strong point of reference within the fashion world.

The foundation contains original concept sketches and technical drawings that provide a fascinating window into the mind of an artistic genius. View a small rotating selection of clothing by the designer. When you see his designs, you can fully understand why Ferré was known as the architect of fashion. Personal items the designer collected during his lifetime help to complete the picture. Ferré travelled widely throughout his lifetime, spent extensive periods of time in India, in particular between 1973 and 1977, and also in China, Japan and the

East, discovering colours and styles that would influence his work. The foundation gathers together some of the artefacts and jewellery he collected. There are also bound volumes, by year, of all the major fashion magazines that Ferré collected from the late 1970s until he died.

The foundation is of particular interest to fashion students and academics and to anyone with more than a general interest in fashion. To visit the foundation, book an appointment by emailing info@fondazioneferre.com

Fondazione Gianfranco Ferré, Via Tortona, 37, 02 3658 0109, Mon-Thurs 9.30 am - 1 pm, 2 pm - 6 pm; Fri 9.30 am - 1 pm, 2 pm - 4 pm. **www.fondazionegianfrancoferre.com**

GIANFRANCO FERRÉ

Gianfranco Ferré, originally from Legnano near Milan, was an architecture student at the Politecnico di Milano from which he graduated in 1969. During this period he started creating belts and bijoux for the women friends on his course in the 1960s. One of these friends was wearing one of these items one day at the Biffi boutique where she worked. It attracted the attention of Rosy Biffi, always on the lookout for new talent, who later encouraged him to begin designing clothes. Ferré's jewellery and accessories began to be noticed by fashion journalists such as Anna Piaggi and were featured in magazines, and in 1971 he began to design accessories for Walter Albini and Karl Lagerfeld.

In 1974 Ferré produced his first

© Archivio Fondazione Gianfranco Ferré

womenswear collections for Baila and Courlande. The owner of the first one was Franco Mattioli, Bolognese industrialist, who became business partner of the young designer. So in 1978, Ferré and Mattioli founded the Gianfranco Ferré company, with Mattioli. In October of the same year the designer brought his debut signature collection of women's ready-to-wear clothing and accessories at the Hotel Principe de Savoia, which received international attention. A menswear collection followed in 1982, and in 1986 he showed his first couture collection in Rome. He would show haute couture collections for six seasons. During this time Ferré became involved in the foundation of the Domus Academy,

Milan's new Design, Design Management and Fashion Design Postgraduate School, where he led the Clothing Design course until 1989. In 1989 he became Artistic Director for the Women's haute couture, Prêt-à-Porter and Fourrure lines until 1996. After this he dedicated himself to his own company until his death in June 2007. He was appointed President of the Brera Fine Arts Academy in March of the same year.

Ferré was known as 'the architect of fashion' because of the way he brought the principles of architecture to fashion, including an acute sense of spatial awareness and of how clothes occupied space. Fashion journalist Anna Piaggi believed he shared the same gift as Balenciaga, the ability to create lightness from construction. He was also famous for his white shirts: he believed that the white shirt was universal, and the interpretation individual.

SHOPPING

Bottegatre (women's shoes and clothing)

Bottegatre specialises in niche products that are mostly Made in Italy. They have an interesting selection of shoes, in particular, their artisan-made brand Casta e Dolly clogs and sandals, which come in various colours and shades. They also have a selection of clothing and other accessories.

Bottegatre, Via Tortona, 12, 02 2513 4675, Mon–Fri 10.30 am – 7.30 pm, Sat 11.30 am – 7.30 pm. **www.bottegatre.com**

Carmen Veca

CARMEN VECA

'When I arrived at the end of the 1990s, Zona Tortona was very different. There were a few markets, a couple of bars, shops selling classic clothes, but apart from that it was virtually unknown. Then over the years things began to change. The Fuorisalone began and within a very short time it injected new life into the area and brought in a breath of fresh air that was full of creativity. New places began to open: clothes shops, restaurants, bars, hotels, architects and then the icing on the cake was when the fashion world chose to come here. Then in 2015, thanks to Expo, the council began to create the new Darsena and it became a new meeting place. I love being here in Zona Tortona with all my familiar places, and everyone knows where to find me now.'

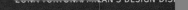

Carmen Veca

Carmen Veca (jewellery)

Carmen Veca has been making jewellery along Via Savona since 1998. She realised she had a passion for jewellery when she did an amateur course in jewellery making. The challenge was to turn it into a job. She started in a small workshop where she sold her designs, and then after a year the shop here became free. Carmen has kept her business small and creates her jewellery with the same passion and love as she always has, and to try to pass this through the pieces she creates. Needless to say, she has clients who have been coming back for years.

Carmen Veca, Via Savona, 1, 02 5810 5363, Tues–Fri 4 – 7 pm (mornings by appointment), Sat 11.30 am – 2 pm, 4 – 7.30 pm.
www.carmenvecamonili.it

Memèm (women's clothing and accessories)

Emanuela Giusti opened Memèm after working in video and photography to pursue her passion for fashion. The result is an eclectic, carefully selected range of women's clothing and accessories, with an emphasis on French designers. Go for a touch of Parisian style, inspired with a touch of the boho.

Memèm, Via Savona, 1, 02 3675 3846, Tues–Sat 10.30 am – 1.30 pm, 3.30 – 7.30 pm. Instagram @memem, Facebook @Memem Via Savona

Nonostante Marras

Enter the fairy-tale world of Antonio Marras, the Sardinian designer and artist from Alghero. His concept store is everything you would expect from the designer whose collections and shows spin theatrical narratives. The whole ambience is as bohemian and romantic as his clothes, vintage furniture, sofas, bookcases, extravagant lighting and flowers. In what used to be a workshop, he puts together clothes, accessories, flowers, a bookshop with art, fashion and design books, a corner dedicated to beauty products, and a bar where you can try typical Sardinian sweets and have an aperitivo in the garden. Marras, known as the most intellectual of Italian designers, fuses design with art and more besides. His first solo art show 'Nulla dies sine linea: life, diaries and notes of a restless man' took place at the Triennale Design Museum in 2016 and involved installations, paintings, drawings, diaries, albums and notebooks.

Nonostante Marras, Via Cola di Rienzo, 8, 02 8907 5002, Tues–Sat 10 am – 7 pm. **www.antoniomarras.com**

SALONE INTERNAZIONALE DEL MOBILE – DESIGN WEEK

In April every year, the Salone Internazionale del Mobile is when Milan becomes a showcase for design brands and products, and the whole city is involved in what's known as Design Week. In 2019, 386,000 people from 181 countries visited this international furniture and design fair held at Milan's Rho Fiera. It's a huge event that includes design exhibitions and installations all around the city by way of its Fuorisalone, while the city's various design districts are in locations such as Brera, the 5 vie district and Isola. Fashion brands also take an active part and organise events and installations that fuse fashion with design, and showcase design in their shops and shop windows. The whole event shows just how the borders between fashion and design are merging as fashion brands move more and more into lifestyle products through new collaborations between fashion and the worlds of art, design and furniture every year. Food also plays its part, with cookery and food events around the city. For details and dates see **www.salonedelmobile.it**

For the Fuorisalone, see **www.fuorisalonemagazine.it**

Milan Design Market

The Milan Design Market gives exposure to emerging designers and creatives who are starting out. You can also buy their creations online. **www.milandesignmarket.it**

LAMBRATE:
Your local neighbourhood, Milanese style

While you wouldn't class Lambrate as a shopping destination, it is your hyper-local neighbourhood with its monthly local festival, 'Il Sabato di Lambrate' or 'the Lambrate Saturday'. It also has one of Milan's best vintage shops, which for any serious vintage fashion lover is reason alone why you should head up there.

Lambrate is in the north east of the city, right next to Città Studi, home to Milan's Politecnico with its prestigious architecture, engineering and design faculties, and news stands full of the latest art and design magazines. Other universities have various faculties there too and the whole atmosphere of the intellectual student life of Città Studi has spilled over into Lambrate and made it one of the places where young people (and not only the young) wish to live. Lambrate's roots, however, are very different. For centuries it was a rural village on the outskirts of Milan near the River Lambro, before it became a centre for Milanese industry in the twentieth century. This was working-class, industrial Milan, home

Giui Rosso, courtesy of Redroom

to Lambretta scooters, Innocenti cars and the Faema coffee machine, symbols of the boom-years' lifestyle of the 1960s. Nowadays it's popular with creatives, another of Milan's previously industrial areas which, like Tortona and Isola, found new life when the creatives began to move into the disused factories and warehouses. Via Ventura is famous for its art galleries, especially the Massimo de Carlo Gallery near the Lambrate station, and Subalterno1, which since it opened in 2011, has become one of the main galleries on a national and European level that specialises in independent Italian design. If you're there during Design Week, make sure it's on your list of districts to visit. It's gained quite a cult status over the years, and some have compared the area to an Italian-style Brooklyn. The whole atmosphere tends to be more relaxed than in other places in Milan, with its open spaces and various food trucks that offer Italian regional specialities and more. In fashion terms, it's a great place to browse the stalls for artisan-made clothing and accessories, and it's an absolute pleasure to do so. (See www.lambratedesigndistrict.com and www.venturaprojects.com for further information.) Also look out for the Luna sign on the corner of Via Ventura and Via Massimiano, which came from the Varesine fairground that was once near Isola before the recent extensive Porta Nuova urban redevelopment project took place.

The best time to head to Lambrate is when the monthly local festival 'Il Sabato di Lambrate' takes place, with its market for artists and local artisans. More than just a market, this is an event organised by people living in a community to contribute to and celebrate that sense of community, with music, art, children's activities, yoga, dancing in the square known by the locals as Piazza Rimembranze di Lambrate, and much more. (For details about the 'Sabato di Lambrate', see Facebook page @sabatodilambrate for dates.) As you're walking along between the stalls of Via Conte Rosso, don't forget to look back for a view of it all with the San Martino church in the background. Milan has many faces, each with its own beauty, and this is one.

EAT AND DRINK

APERITIVO

Birrificio Lambrate

Birrificio Lambrate is Lambrate's own microbrewery where you can chose from beers such as Sant'Ambroeus (Sant'Ambrogio in Milanese dialect).

Birrificio Lambrate, pub, Via Adelchi, 5, 02 7063 8678, Tues–Sun 6 pm – 2 am (restaurant from 8.30 pm); pub/restaurant, Via Golgi, 60, 02 8496 1890, Mon–Fri 12 – 3 pm, 6 pm – 2 am, Sat 7 pm – 2 am (lunch 12 – 3 pm, dinner from 8 pm).

DINNER

Osteria Milano

Head to Osteria Milano for food and live music.

Osteria Milano, Via Gaetano Sbodio, 30, 02 2154 362, bistrot: Tues–Sun 6.30 – 9.30 pm, except Fri–Sat 6.30 – 9.45 pm; restaurant: Tues–Sun 12 – 2.30 pm, 7.30 – 11 pm; cocktail bar Tues–Sun 9.30 pm – 12.30 am, except Fri–Sat 10 pm – 1.30 am.

20134 Lambrate (women's vintage clothing and accessories)

20134 Lambrate is run by Cecilia di Lorenzo and was set up because of her own personal interest and an archive collection she has created over the years. This was followed by another shop, Madame

Rachael Martin

Pauline, with two other business partners (see page 81). 20134 Lambrate specialises in mid-nineteenth-century furniture and vintage clothing, bags, hats, bijoux and shoes that ranges from the early 1900s to the 1970s, with newer pieces. More recent pieces include Prada, Gucci, Marni, Bottega Veneta, Valentino, Gucci and No 21. Look for the 1940s barber's shop sign that's still there, witness to the shop's past.

20134 Lambrate, Via Conte Rosso, 22, 02 9153 3992, Tues–Fri 1 – 7 pm, Sat 11 – 7 pm, although it's recommended that you make an appointment in advance.
www.20134lambrate.it; Instagram and Facebook @20134lambrate_vintage

Redroom

'Handmade Milano Lambrate' reads the sign above the shop, while the reference to Twin Peaks is deliberate. The emphasis is on handmade, design, art and vintage. What links them all is this: originality, sustainability and quality. For Irene Roghi and Andrea Brembati, it's all part of the philosophy behind their shop, which has been open here since 2014. Buy local, buy locally made artisan products, and as part of this they offer courses, workshops and events that are all aimed at gaining a wider audience and telling the story of artisan craftsmanship in Italy today. Look out for

Giui Rosso, courtesy of Redroom

Nicoletta Fasani's women's clothes made in high quality fabrics, Insunsit's magical world of botanical illustrations, BlackMilk bags and accessories, and Petit Pois Rose's illustrated accessories. Then there are Frankie Fabric's knot necklaces, design bijoux using innovative materials by Pig'Oh, wellness and home products, and clothing by Sartoria Ismara and RKR. Their purpose is to give space to emerging artisans and illustrators, both in the shop and within their Red Bazar market that takes place as part of the monthly 'Il Sabato di Lambrate' local festival along Via Conte Rosso.

Redroom, Via Conte Rosso, 18, 02 3012 0481, Tues–Fri 10 am – 1 pm, 4 – 8pm, Sat 12 – 7 pm. **www.redroomstore.com Instagram** @ redroom_store

Lambrate: Irene Roghi and Andrea Brembati

'Lambrate might look like it's always on the move, but its heart likes to retain its traditions. It's like a village that discusses everything that's new, but knows deep down that its soul will always be calm, that its evolution will never be forced because it loves its slow pace and that feeling of time standing still. Or at least that's how we live it all at Redroom. We plan to continue to bring artisans to Via Conte Rosso, the heart of the old Lambrate, with our usual focus on quality, and with the same spirit as our festival. We'd also like to establish links with nearby neighbourhoods such as Rubattino and Ortica, start new events, make use of new spaces, and create new connections with regards to music and theatre. We believe Lambrate offers the tourist something unforeseen, a chance to see a different side of Milan. You can walk amid historic villas but also visit old factory buildings that are no longer in use, browse small shops and artisan workshops. They're all places where the large retailers simply can't compete in terms of history and love for what they do.'

Giui Rosso, courtesy of Redroom

PRACTICAL INFORMATION

KNOW BEFORE YOU GO
Shop opening hours

As a general rule, most shops are closed on Monday mornings, opening at 3.00 or 3.30 pm. On other days they generally open around 10.00 am and close around 7.00 or 7.30 pm, one exception being the Navigli area, where some don't open until the afternoon. Many shops close on Sundays, particularly in areas which are less popular with tourists, and some also stay closed all day on Monday. Some shops also close at lunchtime, especially the smaller ones, so if you're planning on heading off somewhere between the hours of 12 pm and 3.30 pm, check in advance that where you are going doesn't close for lunch. A word about refunds: you will not necessarily be given a refund, so it's always best to ask at the shop before you buy. You should be given the opportunity to exchange goods, although this may differ for sale items. When in doubt, ask before you buy.

Sales

Head to the twice-yearly sales for bargains. Fall/winter collection sales usually begin on 6 January through to February, and spring/summer collections on the first Saturday of July, often until early September.

Seasonal variations in opening hours

While every attempt has been made to ensure that the opening hours are correct, these may be subject to variation, especially around Christmas, and also during the summer months. Times have changed since the whole of Italy shut down in August and headed off to the sea, but saying that, some places do close at some stage during August and shops in the Golden Quad may be closed on Sundays.

Dialling codes

The country code for Italy is 00 39. The Milan prefix is 02. All other numbers refer to mobile phones.

GETTING AROUND

Milan is made up of of nine districts, six of which are named after its six main city gates: Porta Genova, Porta Nuova, Porta Romana, Porta Ticinese, Porta Vigentina and Porta Venezia. The metro is the quickest way to get around, and especially for going from one end of the city to the other. Also consider the tram. You get to see where you are going and it's a great way of seeing Milan and taking in the sights. The 1928 orange Carrelli trams, complete with brass fittings, have become an iconic symbol of the city and make travelling a pleasure in itself. Trams 1 and 33 will show you the major sights. A one-way urban ticket covers central Milan, lasts ninety minutes from when first validated, and costs 2 euro. Alternatively, you can get a One Day Ticket (valid for twenty-four hours after first stamping) or a Two Day Ticket (valid for forty-eight hours after first stamping). Don't forget that you need to stamp your ticket on trams and buses in the machine when you get on, or you could face a fine.

For a journey planner, maps of metro, tram and bus routes with the sights and places of interest marked, go to the **www.atm.it** website and choose ATM Milano official app. Equally, take a look at the Moovit app. Taxis (often white cars), although not cheap, are available on the Uber, Milanotaxi, MyTaxi or AppTaxi apps. You could also consider Milan's bike sharing services. Further details are found on **www.bikemi.com** and **www.mobike.com**

Finally, walk. Milan, like any city, needs to be savoured at leisure. It's how you see those courtyards hidden behind palazzo gates along Corso Venezia, in Brera and in Sant'Ambrogio. Breathe in its history and its culture, absorb that which makes it what it is. Besides, the centre of Milan is not so very big so if you plan your route over the day, you'll be surprised at how much you can see.

THE FASHION LOVER'S LIST: FASHION HOTELS

1. **Armani Hotel** This sleek and stylish hotel above the Armani store is as beautiful as you would expect from the king of elegance himself. The Bamboo Bar there holds the best parties during Milan Fashion Week. Via Alessandro Manzoni, 31, 02 8883 8888.
www.armanihotelmilano.com

2. **Bulgari Hotel** Hidden away down a private street in the heart of the Golden Quad, it's a favourite with the fashion crowd and a hive of activity during Milan Fashion Week. Via Privata Fratelli Gabba, 7b, 02 805 8051.
www.bulgarihotels.com

3. **Baglioni Hotel Carlton** This luxurious boutique hotel is right next to the Golden Quad. Via Senato, 5, 02 77077. **www.baglionihotels.com**

4. **Four Seasons Hotel** Set in what was a fifteenth-century convent, it's a favourite with fashion people such as Anna Wintour and Manolo Blahnik. Via Gesù, 6/8, 02 77088. **www.fourseasons.com**

5. **Grand Hotel et de Milan** Verdi stayed in room 105 and wrote his operas *Othello* and *Falstaff*. Via Manzoni, 29, 02 723141.
www.grandhoteletdemilan.it

6. **Park Hyatt Milan** Reputed to be Milan's number one hotel, this is where Obama stayed when he was in town. Via Tommaso Grossi, 1, 02 8821 1234.
www.hyatt.com

7. **The Yard Hotel** Boutique hotel that's a retake on the gentleman's club and well placed for Porta Ticinese nightlife. Inside there's The Doping Club for cocktails and food. The Yard Hotel, Piazza XXIV Maggio, 8, 02 8941 5901.
www.theyardmilano.com

8. **TownHouse Galleria** is in the Galleria Vittorio Emanuele II with beautiful suites with a view onto the Galleria. Town House Galleria, Via Silvio Pellico, 02 3659 4960. **www.townhousehotels.com**

THE FASHION LOVER'S LIST: OTHER ACCOMMODATION OPTIONS

1. **Bonaparte Suites** Suites and apartments in a beautiful nineteenth century building on Foro Bonaparte near Cadorna station. Foro Buonaparte, 51, 02 8425 9633. **www. bonapartesuites.it**

2. **Casa Base** Part of the multifunctional venue and co-working space that's situated in Tortona. It's popular with creatives visiting the area and offers stays in dormitories or double rooms. The décor is a mix of 1950s and 1960s vintage pieces. Via Bergognone, 34
www.base.milano.it/casabase

3. **LaFavia 4 Rooms** Marco and Fabio have taken inspiration from their world travels for their bed and breakfast complete with rooftop garden. It's located near the Porta Garibaldi station and convenient for Isola, Brera and Corso Como. Via Carlo Farini, 4, 02 784 2212. **www.lafaVia4rooms.com**

4. **Moscova Luxury B&B** Offers modern apartment accommodation with breakfast on Via Moscova between the Garibaldi, Isola and Brera district. Via della Moscova, 27, 338 471 1983. **www.moscovaluxury.com**

5. **Ostello Bello** Offers private rooms and dormitories. Via Medici, 4, 02 3658 2720. **www.ostellobello.com**

6. **T34 Bed and Breakfast** Typical old-style Milanese house that provides country style accommodation in Tortona. Via Tortona, 34, 348 780 0830. **www.t34bb.it**

7. **Un Posto a Milano** Guest house belonging to Cascina Cuccagna that's in the southern Porta Romana area of the city. Via Privata Cuccagna, 2, 02 545 7785.
www.unpostoamilano.it

End Notes

Milan, city of fashion
1. Gnoli, *Moda: Dalla nascita della haute couture a oggi*, p.164
2. Treccani, Maruccelli Germana

Milan Fashion Week
3. Scarpellini, *La Stoffa dell'Italia: Storia e cultura della moda dal 1945 a oggi*, p.54
4. Steele, *Fashion, Italian Style*, p.12
5. Gnoli, *Moda: Dalla nascita della haute couture a oggi*, p.96
6. Gnoli, *Moda: Dalla nascita della haute couture a oggi*, p.104
7. Scarpellini, *La Stoffa dell'Italia: Storia e cultura della moda dal 1945 a oggi*, p.55
8. Gnoli, *Moda: Dalla nascita della haute couture a oggi*, p.168
9. Gnoli, *Moda: Dalla nascita della haute couture a oggi*, p.168
10. Gnoli, *Moda: Dalla nascita della haute couture a oggi*, p.169
11. Gnoli, *Moda: Dalla nascita della haute couture a oggi*, p.170
12. Stanfill, *The Glamour of Italian Fashion since 1956*, p.16
13. Morini, *Storia della Moda: XVIII-XXI secolo*, p.462
14. Vergani, *Maria Pezzi: una vita dentro la moda* p.77

Milan, city of fashion: a historical glance
15. Scarpellini, *La Stoffa dell'Italia: Storia e cultura della moda dal 1945 a oggi*, p.5.
16. Sartorio, D, The Magic World of Curiel, 'Passion, Culture and Beauty'
17. Gnoli, *Moda: Dalla nascita della haute couture a oggi*, p.214 and Vergani, Maria Pezzi: una vita dentro la moda pp.159-160
18. Gnoli, *Moda: Dalla nascita della haute couture a oggi*, p.228

19. Scarpellini, *La Stoffa dell'Italia: Storia e cultura della moda dal 1945 a oggi*, p.136
20. Callahan, *Champagne Supernovas*, p.134

Rosa Genoni
21. Treccani, Genoni Rosa.
22. Frisa, Post-fazione in Soldi, M, Rosa Genoni Moda e Politica: una prospettiva femminista fra 800 e 900

The Golden Quad
23. Cavagna di Gualdana, *La Storia di Milano in 100 Luoghi Memorabili*, p.32
24. Cavagna di Gualdana, *La Storia di Milano in 100 Luoghi Memorabili*, p.3
25. Sartorio, The Magic World of Curiel, 'Family and business, the perfect heritage'

Via Montenapoleone
26. Del Conte, *Risotto with Nettles*, p.10.
27. Sartorio, D, The Magic World of Curiel, 'The exclusivity of elegance'

Via Sant'Andrea
28. Gnoli, Storia della Moda Italiana, Pillole di Dante

BIBLIOGRAPHY

Bellisario, Michaela K., *Guida turistica per Fashion Victim* (Morellini editore, 2008)

Callahan, Maureen, *Champagne Supernovas* (Touchstone, 2014)

Canavari, Rossella and Pistone, Carlotta, *101 Luoghi dove fare Shopping a Milano almeno una volta nella vita* (Newton Compton Editori, 2010)

Casalengo, Carlo, *La Regina Margherita* (Società editrice Il Mulino, 2001)
Cavagna di Gualdana, Giacinta, La Storia di Milano in 100 luoghi memorabili (Newton Compton Editori, 2018

Del Conte, *Risotto with Nettles: A Memoir with Food* (Chatto & Windus, 2009)

Farrauto, Luigi, *Lonely Planet Pocket Milano* (EDT, 2015)

Frisa, Maria Luisa, *Una nuova moda Italiana* (Marsilio-Fondazione Pitti Discovery, 2010)

Frisa, Maria Luisa, Mattirolo, Anna and Tonchi, Stefano Bellissima: L'Italia dell'Alta Moda 1945-1968 (Mondadori Electa, 2014)

Frisa, Maria Luisa, Monti, Gabriele and Tonchi, Stefano *L'Italiana: L'Italia vista dalla moda 1971–2001* (Marsilio Editori, 2018)

Giacomotti, Fabiana, *La Milanese Chic 2014: Guida alla Città dello Stile* (Baldini Castoldi Dalai, 2012, Baldini & Castoldi, 2013)

Gnoli, Sofia, *Moda: dalla nascita della haute couture a oggi* (Carocci editore, 2012)

Lane, David, *The Fashion of these Times: How Italian Style Conquered the World* (Peregrine's Head, 2015)

Lonely Planet Italy 13th edition (Lonely Planet Global Limited, February 2018)

Lonmon, Aylie, *111 negozi di Milano che devi proprio scoprire* (Emons Verlag GmbH, 2015)

Louis Vuitton *City Guide Milan* (Louis Vuitton Malletier, 2018)

Mackerell, Judith *The Unfinished Palazzo*

Margheriti, Gian Luca, *1001 cose da vedere a Milano almeno una volta nella vita* (Newton Compton Editori, 2010)

Mascolo, Olga and Melloni, Alice, *Milano Chic* (Newton Compton editori, 2013)

Milani, Sibilla and Roncari, Emanuela, *Milan Secrets* (Baldini & Castoldi, 2015)

Montani, Stefania and Parigi, Matteo Bini, *Milano su Misura: Craft Shopping Guide* (Gruppo Editoriale, 2013)

Morini, *Enrica, Storia della Moda* (Skira Editore, 2010)

The Rough Guide to Italy 10th edition (Rough Guides, March 2011)

Urbanelli, Elisa (editor), *Schiaparelli & Prada Impossible Conversations* (The Metropolitan Museum of Art, New York, 2012)

Sartoria, Donatella, *The Magic World of Curiel,* Curiel private edition

Scarpellini, Emanuela, *La Stoffa dell'Italia: storia e cultura della moda dal 1945 a oggi* (Gius. Laterza & Figli, 2017)

Shulman Alexandra, *Inside Vogue* (Fig Tree, 2016, Penguin, 2017)

Steele, Valerie, *Fashion, Italian Style* (Yale University Press, 2003)

Stella, Marta, *My Secret Milan: La Milano intima delle Milanesi* (L'Airone, 2013)

Stanfill, Sonnet, *The Glamour of Italian Fashion since 1945* (V&A Publishing, 2014)

Touring Editore, *Milano* (Touring Editore, 2014)

Touring Editore, *Milano: Viaggi d'autore* (Touring Editore in Milano, 1997)

Vergani, Guido, *Maria Pezzi: una vita dentro la moda* (Skira editore, 1998)

Online materials:

Ambrosio, D. (2019) *Le grandi mecenati dell'arte. Luisa Casati, la marches che voleva essere un'opera vivente* Available at: https://www.elle.com/it/magazine/storie-di-donne/a26146755/luisa-casati-collezionista-arte/ (Accessed 13 December 2019)

Archivi della Moda del Novecento, Marucelli, Germana Available at: http://www.moda.san.beniculturali.it/word press/?protagonisti=marucelli-germana-2 (Accessed 12 May 2019)

Associazione Germana Marucelli website Available at: https://associazionegermanamarucelli.org/germana-marucelli/ (Accessed 19 November 2019)
Gnoli, S., Storia della Moda Italiana, Pillole di Dante, online talks. Available at: https://www.youtube.com/watch?v=s7ae1vJJ6YY (Accessed 16 December 2019)

Horwell, V. (2015) *Mariuccia Mandelli obituary* Available at: http://www.theguardian.com/fashion/2015/dec/13/mariuccia-mandelli (Accessed 13 December 2019)

Horwell, V. (2012) *Anna Piaggi obituary* Available at: https://www.theguardian.com/fashion/2012/aug/10/anna-piaggi

Mantovani, V. *Luisa Casati Amman* www.enciclopediadelledonne.it/biografie/luisa-casati-amman

Marazzi, A. (2016) *Anna Piaggi: una visionaria nella moda* Available at: https://www.raiplay.it/programmi/annipiaggi-unavisionarianellamoda

Mazzarella, C (1963) Excerpt from *Gli Amici di Milano* (Accessed 14 December 2019)

MEMOMI La Memoria di Milano, *I pomeriggi al Jamaica* Available at: https://memomi.it/it/0004/164/i-pomeriggi-al-jamaica.html (Accessed 13 December 2019)

MEMOMI La Memoria di Milano, *Racconto di quartiere: Porta Genova* Available at: https://memomi.it/it/00004/49/racconto-di-quartiere-porta-genova.html (Accessed 13 December 2019)

Paniga, M. *Elvira Leonardi Bouyeure* (Biki) Available at: http://www.enciclopediadelledonne.it/biografie/elvira-leonardi-bouyeure-biki/ (Accessed 13 November 2019)

Paulicelli, E. (2017) *Genoni, Rosa* Available at: http://www.treccani.it/enciclopedia/rosa-genoni (Accessed 13 December 2019)

Rossi, G. (2017) *Quel che resta del Sessantotto: la contestazione che cambiò la società* Available at: https://milano.corriere.it/notizie/cronaca/17_luglio_29/sessantotto-contestazione-mostra-lettere-originali-capanna-isec-liceo-parini-12a8aad6-73cb-11e7-a3f5-e19bfc737a80.shtml (Accessed 13 December 2019)

Sorbo, A.M. *Rosa Genoni* Available at: http://www.enciclopediadelledonne.it/biografie/rosa-genoni/ (Accessed 13 December 2019)

The Telegraph, 'Anna Piaggi', (2012) Available at: https://www.telegraph.co.uk/news/obituaries/9467692/Anna-Piaggi.html

Treccani, *Marucelli Germana* http://www.treccani.it/enciclopedia/germana-marucelli_(Dizionario-Biografico)/ (Accessed 19 November 2019)

Treccani, *Veneziani, Jole* www.veneziani.com for Jole Veneziani, (Accessed 13 December 2019)

Vanzetto, C. (2015) *Rosa Genoni, la pioiera del Made in Italy Dalla Valtellina a Parigi* https://www.corriere.it/moda/news/cards/rosa-genoni-pioniera-made-italydalla-valtellina-parigi/prima-scuola-carcere.shtml (Accessed 13 December 2019)

Palumbo, V. (2018) *Maria Pezzi e il racconto della moda* Available at: https://27esimaora.corriere.it/18_maggio_23/maria-pezzi-racconto-moda/ (Accessed 13 December 2019)

The Telegraph, (2015) *Mariuccia Mandelli, Fashion Designer, Obituary* Available at: https://www.telegraph.co.uk/news/obituaries/12062144/Mariuccia-Mandelli-fashion-designer-obituary.html (Accessed 13 December 2019)

Index